LAINIE

A PALMER SISTERS NOVEL 1

KAYT MILLER

This book is a work of fiction. Names, characters, places, and incidents are the product of the author's imagination or are used facetiously. Any resemblance to actual events, locales, or persons, living or dead, is coincidental.

Copyright © 2019 by Kayt Miller

Cover image standard license from Shutterstock.com

Cover Copyright © 2019 Kayt Miller

All rights reserved.

In accordance with the U.S. Copyright act of 1976, the scanning, uploading, and electronic sharing of any part of this book without the permission of the author is unlawful piracy and theft of the author's intellectual property. If you would like to use material from the book (other than for review purposes), prior written permission must be obtained by contacting the author @ kaytmiller1@yahoo.com. Thank you for your support of the author's rights.

 Created with Vellum

CONTENTS

Dedication	v
Chapter 1	1
Chapter 2	9
Chapter 3	19
Chapter 4	27
Chapter 5	35
Chapter 6	43
Chapter 7	49
Chapter 8	57
Chapter 9	65
Chapter 10	69
Chapter 11	77
Chapter 12	87
Chapter 13	89
Chapter 14	97
Chapter 15	107
Chapter 16	115
Chapter 17	129
Chapter 18	137
Chapter 19	145
Chapter 20	151
Chapter 21	163
Chapter 22	171
Chapter 23	177
Chapter 24	183

Books by Kayt Miller	193
Acknowledgments	195
About the Author	197
Cover Design	199
Thank you!	201
Sneak Peek: Agatha	203

DEDICATION

*To all of my girlfriends who keep me laughing and sane
(well, sort of).
&
To my mom, the strongest person I know.*

CHAPTER ONE

Lainie

"I'M SO NERVOUS." *How did I talk myself into this? This was a terrible idea.* I pound my head (lightly) against my steering wheel, doing my darndest to get out of the car and walk into that shop to do what I set out to do. Pulling in a breath for courage, I decide to change my mantra to something that will actually help me get my big buttocks out of this vehicle. So, here goes. *You can do this, Lainie. You've been thinking about this for weeks.* (Well, two weeks, but that's weeks. Right?) *You've done your due diligence.* And by that, I mean I surveilled this place like a common criminal. But at least I know what I'm walking into. "Open the dang car door, Lainie. You. Can. Do. It."

I push open the door to the old blue Honda I borrowed from my baby sister. It creaks so loudly, it's like it's screaming in pain. Well, it might be. Bessie's old. I got her when I was sixteen, and she was old back then. I gave her to Keely ten years ago because I didn't need her anymore—you know, since I was going to be married. Forever. Ha! That's a joke. Luckily, Keely has kept her running by sheer will alone—oh, and a little duct tape.

Stepping one pink Mary Jane wedge onto the ground, I hesitate. "You've got this, Lainie," I whisper under my breath. Lifting myself up, I place the other foot on the ground beside the first one. Looking down at my feet, I smile. "Gosh, I love these shoes." I reach back into the car to grab my purse, my notebook and pen inside, but it's no longer on the passenger seat. I scan the small space and spot it on the floor in front of the seat. I slide further into the car and reach until my fingertips brush against the handle.

"Well, hello, sweetheart."

I freeze momentarily, then turn my head to see a big, blond, Thor-like man looking down at my backside. I look back at what he sees and squeak. *Great. Just great.* I'm showing a lot of skin and a sliver of white granny panty. Scooting out of the car, I push down my blue dress with the pink polka dots. "Oh, um, yes. Hello."

Before I can say another word, he jumps in, nodding down at Bessie. "You know, we only work on bikes here, but for you, I'd make an exception." He tops it off with a wink and a smirk.

He's cute. *Really* cute. But I'm not here to gawk at men. I'm here to work. *Right. Get on with it, Lainie.* "I'm here to interview—"

"An interview?"

"Yes, I—"

"Well, then, beautiful, you're going to want to talk to Keeton."

"Keeton?" *Beautiful?*

"Keeton Gustafson. The owner."

"Oh, right. The owner. Keeton. Yes, I'd like to speak with him. Keeton. The owner." Geesh, I'd like to slap my own dang self. *Shut up, Lainie. You sound like you were dropped on your head as a child.* Clearing my throat, I watch him turn and take steps toward the huge brick building, so I follow the big hunk. I can't help being mesmerized by his round bottom and muscular thighs. Mm, I love muscular thighs. My ex? He didn't have muscular thighs. Or muscular anything, for that matter.

"Do you always repeat people?"

I'm pulled from my memories of Lewis, my ex. "Huh? What?"

"I said. Do you always repeat people?"

"Repeat people?" What is he talking about?

He starts to chuckle, and it's a nice, deep rumbling sound. Ooh, that was good. *Deep rumbling sound.* I need to write that down. As I walk, I start to dig through my purse for that pen. I guess I'm not paying attention, because the guy stops suddenly and I run right into him. "Oops, sorry." Gosh, I'm such a dork.

"No problem. You can bump that curvy little body against me anytime."

I blush. I know I do, because I feel the heat rise up from my chest into my cheeks. I'm not used to people saying things like that to me. Men, especially. I mean, I'm not tragic-looking or anything, but I'm also no model. God, what am I saying? I'd have to lose about eighty pounds to walk the catwalk. I give myself an internal eyeroll. *Yeah, like that'd ever happen.* No matter how many times Lewis signed me up for gyms and weight loss programs in the ten years we were married, it never worked. Actually, I think I *gained* weight—caused primarily by stress eating. The stress of trying to be something I'm not for a man who was all about appearances.

Shaking my head, I look back up at the blond giant. "What did you say your name was again?"

"I didn't." He smirks. "It's Eric."

"Eric," I repeat.

He chuckles again. "What's yours?"

"My name?"

He nods.

"Lainie."

"Okay, come on, beautiful Lainie. Let's go see the boss man."

There he goes with the "beautiful" again. I bet he says that to all the ladies. He's got player written all over him. Ignoring his sexy-suave comments, I follow him past three open garage bays that look very tidy. Actually, the place looks squeaky clean. Peeking further inside, I see several people walking around and another few working on motorcycles doing whatever it is they do here. It sure looks like they're busy. People come and go from this place all day long. One night, when I was just passing by (wink, wink), I noticed they were having a party. People were dressed up in suits and cocktail attire holding champagne glasses, milling around the parking lot and even in those garages. I was itching to crash that party just to find out the occasion. Maybe I'll ask about that today.

We pass one door and stop at a second one. He opens it. "Thank you, Eric."

"You're *very* welcome."

Even the way he says "very" is filled with innuendo.

He motions me inside ahead of him, so I step through the door and halt. It's some kind of showroom. A large showroom. It must be a hundred feet square or more.

"Keep moving, sweetheart."

Oh, I stopped right in the entrance. Eric can't get past me. "Right." I walk in further and stop, letting Eric pass.

"This is Keeton's brag room."

"Brag room?"

"Yeah, well, look around. These are his awards, and he's got every magazine cover he's ever graced framed on the walls." He points to the far end of the room at a motorcycle. "That's his first custom bike right there. He won't part with it for any amount of money." He looks down at me. "You hang here for a minute. I'll go see if Keeton's got time to see you."

"Alright. I'll just look around." The first thing I notice is the overall feel of the place. Cool. Steely. That's most likely due to the color scheme of black with various shades of gray. There are metallic things all around the space too, in the picture frames and some of the furniture pieces. I see spots of yellow here and there as well. In the lounge area, there's a matching set of black leather furniture decorated with yellow throw pillows. A glass-top coffee table that looks like it's made from chrome exhaust pipes is between those three furniture pieces, and there's a large flat-screen television on the wall facing the lounge area. To the right is what looks like a kitchenette made out of the kind of storage cupboards a person would use in their garage or man cave. The cupboard fronts are covered with textured metal, giving it an industrial feel. It even has a fridge, sink, and what looks to be a state-of-the-art coffee machine. If I was writing about that coffee machine, I'd call it futuristic.

I look to my left at a little niche that holds a large drafting table with a lamp, a stool, and a tall organizer. As I approach, I see a drawing sitting on top of a motorcycle. There are art supplies strewn about on the table as well. The closer I get, the more detail I see. The drawing of the machine is beautiful. The bike looks almost as futuristic as the coffee maker—like a spaceship shaded in blues and purples. Closer still, and I see a signature on the bottom of the drawing. *Keeton*. That's all it says.

I walk slowly around the room, looking at the framed magazines on my way over to the first motorcycle. I get as close as I can, but it's actually roped off. I guess he doesn't want anyone touching it. The little placard resting on the seat says *Don't touch my fucking bike!—Keeton*. Yeah, that's a dead giveaway. I don't blame him. The thing is beautiful. I don't think there's another word for it. It's not black or silver, it's both. If I tilt my head just a little, it looks silver. Another way, black. I wonder how he did that? The bike is huge too. If the seat were slightly larger, I bet you'd get three people on the back of it. Or two of me. The handlebars, if you can call them that, look like they're part of the gas tank. *How do you steer that thing?*

A huge poster hangs above the bike. It looks like a magazine cover that was blown up for just this spot. Across the top it says *Motorworld*. Below that is a picture of this motorcycle. But that's not what catches my eye. It's the man standing behind it. He's unbelievable. I've never seen a man like that. Big, muscled, tattooed, and *beautiful*. I even say that word breathlessly in my head. His arms are crossed in front of him, causing his muscles to bulge extra big. I step as close as I can in an attempt to get a closer look at his tattoos. It's difficult—there are a lot of them. I believe they call that a sleeve. When I look at his face, I gasp. He's magnificent. There's no other word to describe it. He's clean-shaven, which is good, because if he had a beard it'd cover up that strong chin and squarish jaw and hide those amazing lips. He's smiling in the photo, revealing straight teeth, but it also makes his bright blue eyes crinkle at the corners. He looks to be in his thirties like me. I wonder when this cover was done. I search the image for a date but can't find one. I read the rest of the text aloud, "Keeton Gustafson just grabbed custom motorcycle design by the balls."

Wow, I'm not sure what that means exactly, but I'm going to guess it's a good thing. I look back at the man and stare at his hair. Blond. Well, dirty-blond streaked with lots of other blond hues, probably thanks to the sun. Not only that, it's long—much longer than mine, so past his shoulders. Long enough to put in one of those man buns. "I love man buns," I sigh.

Just as I'm about to force myself away from the poster, I hear Eric's voice. "Hey, sweetheart, you can come back here now."

I walk to the entrance of the hallway Eric took earlier. I see him standing in front of a door at the end, so I head his way, all the while looking at more framed images. This batch are of this shop.

At the doorway, Eric steps aside, and I step in and nearly faint. It's *him*. Keeton. Only his hair isn't long anymore. I'd be sad about it if he weren't even more breathtaking without it. He's perfect. My heart is pounding so hard in my chest, I'm sure both men can hear it. Sweat has suddenly appeared at my hairline and my palms. I wipe my hands on my skirt as discreetly as possible. No way do I want him to know I'm about to wrap myself around him like a koala on a tree. Inwardly, that visual makes me giggle. Outwardly? Not so much.

I watch as he stands, holding his hand out. "Keeton Gustafson."

Holy moly, his voice. I felt that deep rumble all the way down to my bright pink toes. This man is dangerous. He could very well be my undoing.

CHAPTER TWO

KEETON

I'M GROWLING at the computer that won't do what the fuck I want it to do when I hear a knock on my office door. "It'd better be good," I shout.

"Oh, it is, brother" comes a voice from the other side. A voice I recognize.

"It's open."

The door clicks open, and my little brother Eric steps in, shutting the door quickly. "Someone's here to do an interview."

I blink a few times. "What? I didn't agree to any interviews." I'm going to kill (or fire) our PR firm. "I don't have time. I'm trying to sort out Molly's bookkeeping shit. Her way of doing things makes no sense to me. I'm fucking it all up. When she gets back—"

"*If* she comes back."

"Don't say it." My little sister had better not bail on us here.

"*When* she comes back from maternity leave, she's going to be pissed."

"Which is why she may not come back. She'll see all the damage you've caused and—"

"Hey. It's not just me, *Eric*." Eric has been in here digging through shit, leaving papers and invoices strewn everywhere. It's not just me.

Eric sighs. "Anyway, you're gonna want to talk to this one."

I run my fingers over the top of my head. I miss my hair. I got a burr up my ass last weekend and cut it all off. I'd grown it out halfway to my ass, but it was annoying me. My regret is offset by the knowledge that I donated it all. *That* was worth it. Besides, I've still got a couple inches of hair on the top, but the sides are short as hell. "Why do I want to talk to this one? Enlighten me."

"You're going to like her."

"Like her?"

"She's just your type."

"I don't have a type." Not anymore. Women are trouble and a pain in my ass. My sister, Molly, and my ex-wife, Deb, are the exceptions. I'll cut Molly some slack, and not because she's my sister. She's had it rough and she's weathered it like a champ. As for Deb? She's always been cool. A better friend than a wife, for sure.

"You will after you see her."

"Jesus, Eric. Just send her in." I need to see what he's talking about. He's full of shit most of the time, but at twenty-five, he's still too young to know better. I sit stock-still at Molly's desk, which is no longer neat and tidy like Molly likes it. Yeah, she's going to kill us.

Eric steps out into the hallway and calls, "Hey, sweetheart, you can come back here now."

When I hear the click-clack of women's shoes, I look up and

see her. Well, damn. I start at the prissy pink shoes and let my eyes travel up her legs. She's got great fucking legs. At her knees, a blue skirt with pink polka dots appears. I follow that up past wide hips and a belt that is cinching her in at the middle. The belt might be too tight, since there's extra curves just above it. Her chest, damn, her chest is spectacular, although I can't see any cleavage because she's got her top buttoned almost all the way up to her neck. The top is blue to match the skirt, with fluffy short sleeves. She reminds me of a woman from the 50s. Well, pictures of women from the 50s. I linger another second on her chest, then move up to her face. My breath catches. Goddamn, she's pretty. Her hair is dark. I usually go for blondes, so Eric was wrong about that part. Everything else, though, yeah. Fuck yeah. Her dark hair is short, hitting just below her ears. There are big curls and waves that look as soft as her skin; she keeps it all neatly tucked behind her ears. It looks thick and shiny, but that's not the appealing part. It's her.... Well, her entire face looks like it came off an angel. Full, dark pink lips. A dainty nose between big eyes that look to be hazel. I can't quite make out the color due to her thick glasses. I stand and raise my hand to shake hers. "Keeton Gustafson."

She blinks at me, giving me a small smile. Raising her hand, she takes mine and shakes quickly, returning her tiny hand back to her side, "Lainie Palmer-Bottoms."

Palm her bottom? That's got to be a joke. "Lainie Palmer-Bottoms? Really?"

"Yes. Why?"

"That's a mouthful." Oh, yeah, she is.

"Well, Bottoms is my married name. Or it *was,* when I was married. I hyphenated my maiden name so it wasn't forgotten. You know, when or if.... Anyway, I'm thinking about dropping the last name. You know? The divorce is fairly recent. So, um, yeah."

I watch as she fidgets. She's nervous. "Are you new at this job?" I can't believe they'd send a rookie to interview me. It's sort of insulting.

She rolls her eyes. "So new. You can tell?"

"You seem nervous."

"I am. I'm sorry." She looks down at the piles of papers on Molly's desk. "Oh, you look busy. I can come back another time."

"Nah, now's as good a time as any." It really isn't a good time; I'm busy as hell. I've got a new project I should have started last week but here I am, doing Molly's work. But little Lainie is here, and she looks so pretty. I wonder what she smells like. Whatever it is, I bet it's sweet as fuck. "Have a seat." I point to the only other chair in Molly's tiny office.

"All right." She pulls out the chair from its spot up against the desk. Bending down, she picks up something. Upright again, I see she's holding a stack of papers and parts catalogs.

I reach out and take them from her, looking all around the office for a spot that isn't already covered in our mess. Finding a small section of a filing cabinet, I set them there. Sitting back down in my chair, I lean back and place my hands behind my head. "So, where's this going to be published?"

"Oh, um, online?"

She's not sure? "Online?"

"Yes. Maybe some other places too."

"You freelance?"

"I guess." She shrugs.

She guesses? "So, ask away." The sooner we get started, the sooner I can get back to work.

"Right." She flips open her notebook and clicks her pen to life. "What is the name of your MC?" She looks up at the walls of the office. "I don't see your logo or anything."

"My MC?"

"Yeah, you know, your motorcycle club."

"This isn't an MC. We're a custom motorcycle shop. We restore vintage bikes and build bikes from scratch. Creative bikes."

"You're only a bike shop?"

"Yeah." *Only?* I chuckle.

"And you're not a motorcycle club?"

"No."

"But, I've seen people, guys mainly, coming in and out of this place in leather cuts."

"And?" She's seen people coming in and out? What's she been doing? Casing the joint?

"Well, shoot." She closes her notebook and looks up at me. "I think there's been some kind of mistake."

Not from where I'm sitting. "How so?"

She doesn't get a chance to answer that because the phone rings just then. Holding up my finger, I pick it up. "GCM. Keeton." I pause and listen to one of our vendors. "It's late?" Shit. I forgot to pay the company that provides our mufflers. "Hang on." I set the phone on top of the pile of papers and turn to the computer. I must have bumped something, because my screen goes blank. Well, not the computer, but the Excel worksheet I had open is gone. What remains is a blank form. "Fuck," I grumble.

I move the mouse to the tab at the top that reads File, open it so I can do a search, but when I type in the company name, there's nothing there. "Goddamn piece of crap," I mutter to myself.

"Can I help you?" Her sweet voice startles me out of my frustration.

"Only if you know Excel."

"I know a little bit."

I push my chair back and point at the computer. "I need to find the invoice or whatever for J&D Cycle Parts."

"Okay." She steps in front of me tentatively. Looking back at me, she turns toward the computer, bending at the waist. It causes her ass to come into full view right before my eyes. My fingers twitch to touch. I'm so distracted I almost miss her question. "What was the name again?"

Shaking off my momentary lust-filled thoughts, I repeat, "J&D Cycle Parts."

I hear her click around and watch her hips move, just a little bit, from side to side as she types. "Is this it?"

She stands up, moving to her left, pointing at the screen. I roll my chair up and almost wrap my arm around her hips like it belongs there or something. Looking up at her, I get a whiff of her scent. Girly. Flowery. But not overdone. It's subtle. Damn, it makes me hard. Peering at the screen, I smile. "Shit. Yes."

Picking up the phone again, I say, "Sorry. Molly's on maternity leave, and I don't know shit about Excel. We found the invoice. I'll get the payment in the mail—" I'm stopped by the woman on the other end. "I pay online? How the fuck...?"

"I'll help you," Lainie Palmer-Bottoms whispers.

"I've got someone here who can do it. I'll send it in a few." I listen to the woman thank me even though I can tell by her tone she's unhappy. We hang up, and I smile. "You saved my ass."

"Well, I'm sure you would have figured it out."

Oh, she's one of those. A bright-side-of-lifer. I grunt, "No. But I can't help wondering who else I stiffed last month."

Lainie blushes and it makes me smile. *Stiffed*. She's got a dirty mind. I like that. "Let's get back to the interview so I can continue fucking up Molly's entire system."

"Right." She sits back down and gets into position. "So, you aren't a motorcycle club." Opening up her little notebook, she jots something down. Without looking up at me she asks, "So, does that mean you all don't have old ladies?"

I'm struck dumb by her question, but I shake my head. "No. We don't call our partners and wives by that moniker."

"Oh, you're married?"

She sounds disappointed. Sweet. "Divorced. Just like you." I smirk. But it occurs to me. These are strange questions. "Why is some online rag interested in my shop? I don't get why you're interviewing me."

"Your shop?" She blinks her pretty lashes at me. "No. I, oh, I guess I didn't really explain."

I wait, but she must be doing the same thing. "Explain what?"

She laughs. "I'm writing a book, silly. About a biker gang and their old ladies."

Silly? I bet she says golly-gee-willikers too. "What kind of book? I mean, is it nonfiction?" If so, she's barking up the wrong tree.

"No, it's fiction." She leans forward like she's going to share a secret. "A romance."

"A romance?" What the hell is she doing here with me? There's not one fucking romantic thing about me. Just ask my ex-wife. Hell, ask all of my past girlfriends.

"Yes," she whispers, "a *steamy* romance."

"Steamy, huh? So, lots of fucking and whatnot?" See? Not romantic.

She turns a pretty shade of pink that I like very much. "Sure. I guess that's one way of putting it."

I could put it in a whole other way, but the fucking phone rings again. "GCM. Keeton." I listen to the vendor on the line and squeeze my eyes shut. Another nonpayment phone call. "When was it due?"

As I listen, I watch little miss steamy romance stand up and walk around the desk to her spot in front of the computer. This time I don't move much. Her leg brushes against mine, and my cock nearly punches out of my jeans. This woman is driving me crazy. From her bent position, she turns to look at me. Goddamn, if I could only lift that skirt up.... "What's the name?" she whispers.

"Hang on a sec, Kate." I place my palm over the receiver. "Force Tires."

I watch her click around on the computer. "Aha!" She stands, turning to face me, a smug little smile on her face. "Is this it?"

I peer around her, letting my eyes scan her tits again. Damn, they're stellar. "Yep." Placing the receiver back over my mouth, I say, "Got it. I'll take care of it today." Hanging up the phone, I watch her return to her seat.

"So, you don't know anything about motorcycle clubs?" she asks.

"Well...."

"Do you know anyone in a motorcycle club who'd talk to me?"

I blink, picturing her talking to some criminal. I don't like it. "A friend of mine rides with a club. John." He's not really who she wants to talk to, though. He's a dentist, and his *old lady* is a pediatrician. I don't think that's what she's after.

"John? Seriously? Not Snake or Axle?" She looks up. "Ooh, or what about *Viper*?" Her voice is breathy saying "Viper," like it's some kind of cookie.

If I wasn't completely dumbstruck, I'd probably laugh, but she's serious.

"What's the name of his club? Please tell me it's something like Satan's Crew."

Now I laugh. "Jesus, woman. You really are imaginative, aren't you?"

That makes her smile for the first time, and it takes my breath away. She smiles everywhere, from her twinkling hazel eyes down to her gorgeous pink lips. Her teeth are straight and white. I'm about to reach out and pull her onto my lap when my fucking phone rings again. Before I can answer it, my pretty friend picks it up. "GCM. This is Lainie. How may I help you?"

Wow, she sounds professional. Standing up, she gestures for me to move back. This time, I only turn my seat, so she has to step between my legs to get to my computer. Yeah, a little creepy, but this shit has gone on long enough. I lean forward just enough to smell her again. It's killing my cock, but it can't be helped.

"Yes? Can you repeat the name of your company again, please?" She types. "Uh-huh." She types some more. "Right. Got it. I'm so sorry it's late. Our normal office manager is on maternity leave, and we're just getting caught up."

She stands, placing her hand on her hip. Her nails are short, but they're painted in a pretty pink shade. I bet lots of her is a pretty pink color. I should design a bike that color. And give it to her. My dick is fucking painful now that I've pictured her in a leather miniskirt and black tank on her hot pink bike. Damn it. I've got to get the hell out of here. Standing up fast, I place my palm on her waist. Leaning in to her phoneless ear, I whisper, "Back in a few minutes, Lainie." I hear a little gasp and feel a tiny shiver run through her. I *really* need to get out of here to ease some of this tension. I step away from her to the door, adjusting myself as I go. In the hallway, I make a beeline for the bathroom.

"Told you she was your type."

"Shut the fuck up, Eric. Get back to work."

"Yes, boss. But if you're going to be a while in there"—he nods to the bathroom—"I can take over the interview."

"Don't even think about it," I growl.

I listen as his chuckle grows quieter the further away he gets. If I weren't about to bust a nut, I'd laugh. Stepping into the bathroom, I rub my palm over my hard-on. I shouldn't do that. It makes it worse. "Think about baseball," I grumble to myself. "Or taxes." Anything that will help make this thing go down, not up. Pumping some hand soap into my palm, I wash my hands and splash cold water on my face. Looking down, I see my cock running down the inside of my leg. At least it had somewhere to go, even though it makes it difficult to walk. Or sit.

Squeezing my eyes shut, I picture my new friend, Lainie, spread out, naked on my desk, legs open, her pretty pink pussy on display just for me. "Mine," I groan. I let my imagination's eyes move up, picturing her glorious tits bouncing as I fuck the bejesus out of her. "Lainie." I moan.

Then I hear it. A tiny gasp. Looking to my left, I see the door is ajar. I guess I didn't shut it all the way, and the woman who's caused my current state is standing just outside. Her eyes are on my jeans and my obvious hard-on. Her face is the same color as her nail polish now. I can tell because her hand is over her mouth. She's shocked, but she's not moving.

"You like what you see, little Lainie?" I ask gruffly. Yeah, I'm a dick.

"No," she barely whispers.

"No? It sure looks like it." She says nothing. Having her check me out is making me harder than I've ever been. Placing my palm over my jeans, I attempt to adjust myself. "Say my name, Lainie."

"Keeton," she says in the sweetest voice ever created.

"Fuck, woman. You're too good to be true." I wish I could keep her. But, that can't happen. Or it *shouldn't* happen. I'm not the man for her.

CHAPTER THREE

Lainie

WHAT JUST HAPPENED? Oh, I know. I, Lainie Palmer-Bottoms, just gawked at a man's erection. A man I only just met. A man, from the looks of it, has a very impressive penis. I should feel terrible, scandalized, guilty even, but I don't. I feel exhilarated. It's exactly the kind of experience I need for my book. I mean, I've got none of my own to write about.

I guess now's the time to tell you that you're talking to the world's one and only divorced virgin. Are you confused? The truth is, I'm a thirty-one-year-old divorced woman who never had sex with her husband. My gay husband. Okay, I'm probably not *technically* a virgin anymore thanks to several BOBs (battery operated boyfriends) in my nightstand drawer. BOB number one took care of my pesky hymen my first year of marriage. I've added new BOBs along the way because, well, I've *needed* them.

Before you pity me, you should know I was well aware of his

preferences before I married him. Honestly? I was thrilled to be the first of my friends to marry at the ripe old age of twenty. It meant that I was no longer the single, fat friend who people felt sorry for; I was part of a couple. Something I'd never been before. Which meant I never had to go to a wedding or party alone again. Well, at least that's what I thought. It turns out Lewis only went to parties and events that helped his career along. You see, he works for a very conservative bank. A bank that wouldn't appreciate the fact that he likes other men. I, for one, think it's ridiculous. He's a grown man. He should be able to love who he wants, but that's not how the world works, I guess.

The thing about Lewis Bottoms, though, is that not only is he gay, he's also a controlling, elitist snob who did everything he could to micromanage every aspect of our life. *My* life. He wanted me to be the perfect wife. That included everything from my body and what I wore and ate to how I cleaned the bathroom. At first I thought that's what marriage was—two people trying to make each other better—but it turns out that it was only one person dictating how to make the other one better. Better according to him. By about the third year, I started to become resentful. I didn't want Lewis to know how I was feeling, because making him angry was not what I wanted. Lew could be a real a-hole. Instead, I became rather passive-aggressive. I did things like playing the opposites game with him. For example, if he told me to wear black to a party, I'd wear red or white. If, while we were out to eat with clients or business associates and he tried to order for me, I'd raise my little finger to the server and tell them, "Excuse me. I changed my mind. I'd like the deep-fried *whatever* is on the menu." His jaw would clench, and his teeth would grind, but I'd just smile and play the doting, obedient wife. He always had a meltdown once we got home. At first, I'd listen. Occasionally he'd make me cry saying mean things about my body, but after too many times of that happening, I'd just ignore him, walk into my bedroom, and shut the door on him and his wrath.

Strangely, it was Lewis who wanted the divorce. I don't know if he decided to come out to people at his job or what. The catalyst that caused him to file for divorce is a mystery, and since I haven't talked to him since before his lawyer served me with papers, I may never know. I signed the papers lickety-split without even reading them, which was a terrible mistake. I got essentially nothing in the divorce. I kept my clothes and the gifts he gave me, what there were of those. I don't even have a car in my name, hence me driving Keely's beater.

Honestly, I was relieved to get the papers. I didn't have the courage to do it myself. A big reason for that related to money. Lew is well-connected. If I'd gone to one locally, he would have heard about it. If I went to say, Flagstaff, I would have had to pay an arm and a leg for a good attorney and since Lewis insisted he control most of the money.... I say most because in about year four, I told him I wanted to get a part-time job. He flew into such a dramatic rage I nearly caved. See? Control. But this time I told him I needed to earn my own money. After that, he started giving me an allowance. Can you believe that? No matter, I used the allowance to finish my English degree, online, that I'd started before we were married. Interestingly, he doesn't know about that. I've kept it from him all this time.

I also invested some of the money. I learned about investments from listening to Lewis and his colleagues. I'd make little notes to myself after dinners and cocktail parties about companies and investments that were hot or showed promise. It's thanks to those men thinking I was too daft to take advantage of the tips that helped me make some smart moves, giving me some cushion right now. Not enough cushion to buy my own house or a brand-new car, but enough to find my own apartment and when I get the chance, a used car. For now, paying half of my sister, Keely's, rent helps her out a little bit while I figure my life out.

I know what you're thinking—you're wondering why I stayed, right? The answer is simple. I was raised to believe that marriage was a commitment, even if there was no sex. I cared about Lewis, mostly, warts and all, but it was never romantic love, obviously. No, I get all the sexy romantic love I want from books (and porn). *Wink.*

I must have been lost in thought, because I'm brought back to the scene before me as he, Keeton Gustafson, touches me. That's right. The hottest man I've ever laid eyes on has just brushed his finger across my cheek. I hold my breath as his thumb swipes gently over my bottom lip.

"You're a fucking wet dream, Lainie Palmer-Bottoms."

"M-me?" He can't be serious.

"Why does that surprise you? You were married, right? And what? He didn't worship you? Is that why you left him?"

Where do I start with all of that? *"He* left *me."* I guess there's that.

"What a fucking idiot." He's moved even closer to me. I feel his breath on my face. His, how shall I say, *penis* is still hard. I can feel it pressed against me. I should probably skedaddle, but I can't. This is great material for my book. I need to go with it.

"It wasn't a con-conventional marriage." I'm shivering so much I can't get the words out.

"How so, baby?"

Baby? OMG! I love it when the Hero, big H, calls the heroine baby. L-o-v-e, love it.

His hands are sort of everywhere. The one that was touching my face is now behind my head, on the back of my neck. His other one is rubbing circles on my waist and hip. Ordinarily I'd flinch at anyone touching my love handles, but for some reason, it doesn't bother me this time. Clearing my throat, I confess, "He was gay. My husband was gay."

"What?!" He steps back, away from me, and I feel the loss. "He fucking married you, then he told you he was gay?"

"Not exactly."

"Not exactly?"

This is so embarrassing. "Look. I don't want to talk about it, okay. It's not really any of your—" Before I can finish he's back, but closer—so close his lips are on mine in a hungry, possessive kind of kiss. The kind of kiss I've only read about.

I must be stiff as a board, because he pulls back, whispering in a deep, raspy voice. It's sexy as all get-out. "Open your mouth for me, sweet girl."

"Oh" is all I get out before his mouth is on mine again. His tongue sweeps inside so sensually. It brushes against mine quickly, then deeper and more ravenously. I should probably stop it. This kiss, I mean. It's inappropriate. Probably. But in all my thirty-one years, no one has ever felt compelled to just kiss me. It's like a scene from a book. For the first time in my life, I'm not going to let propriety get in the way of this experience, because trust me when I say, This. Man. Can. Kiss.

His palm moves from my hip to my ass, pressing me closer to him. It seems impossible that there was any room at all. What also seems impossible is the fact that his giant penis feels like it's getting bigger. But that can't be. Right?

Keeton slows the kiss down until he's giving me soft, sweet kisses on the corner of my mouth, my cheek, forehead, below my ear. Oh, now that one gave me tingles all the way down. If you know what I mean.

"So fucking sweet," he mumbles. "Too damn sweet for me." Stepping away from me, Keeton winces as he adjusts himself. "Wish I had some sweatpants." He chuckles.

"Why did you do that?" I ask absently. I'm still trying to figure out what he meant by "too sweet for me."

"Do what?"

"Kiss me. Why'd you kiss me?" It was so out of the blue.

He's looking me in the eye, and it's a tad unnerving. "I couldn't help myself. You're the most beautiful woman I've ever seen in my life. I had to know."

"Know?" What is he talking about? *The most beautiful woman?* "What did you have to know?"

"I had to know if your lips were as sweet as I imagined."

Oh. Dang. I want to ask him if they *were* as sweet as he imagined. Instead, I just look at his handsome face, then down at my feet. My face heats again.

"The answer is no." Hurt flushes through my body. I'm about to cut and run when he adds, "It was sweeter."

My eyes are back up peering into his. "Oh."

I watch him turn and walk away gingerly and wonder, *what happens next?* Are we dating now? I laugh out loud this time. I mean, that was a funny thought. I'm shocked by my own naiveté sometimes.

"Are you laughing at my plight?"

"No. I, oh, never mind." I walk past him into his office to grab my purse. "I guess I should get going." I mean... there's no reason to stay. He's not in a motorcycle club, so he really can't give me tips and feedback about the lifestyle. But, *that kiss*. That kiss could star in my book. Maybe I'll end up getting more real-life experience writing this book.

What? It could happen.

"Sure. See you."

"Right. See you." What a weird day. I step around him and out of his office. I force myself to look ahead. *No looking back.* At this moment, I'm taking it very literally. Just as I start to pull the door open, the phone rings. I hear Keeton muttering profanities. I hesitate. Should I help him? I did forget to show him how to pay those bills online.

I'm just about to keep going when Keeton's head appears from inside the office. "Lainie!" he shouts. "Thank fuck you're still here. Can you help me one more time?"

Sighing, I give him a little smile. "Sure." I mean, the guy gave me my first real kiss. (And no, Lewis's tiny peck on my lips at the altar doesn't count.) I can do something for him too.

CHAPTER FOUR

KEETON

BY THE TIME she's finished showing me how to search for invoices the easy way and instructed me how to pay my bills through PayPal, I feel better. Not enough to know I can handle this and do my custom work too. No, something's got to give. Molly had the baby a few weeks ago. She'll be gone at least another five. By then, I'll have majorly fucked up her system. So much so, I'm sure she'll never speak to me again.

There's also the risk that she won't come back at all. She's a single mom now. Her baby daddy is out of the picture. Dead. Afghanistan. A week before he was due to come home for good and three weeks before Madalyn was born. And goddamn, it hurts. I loved Adam like a brother. Hell, we were friends before the two of them even met. He was good to her, treated her like a princess, and she was perfect for him too. It fucking sucks. So, no, I wouldn't blame her for staying home and loving her baby like Adam would have wanted. She'll have his pension and other benefits, which she'll need, but it doesn't make up for the fact that her man is gone.

I swallow down the sadness. I don't want Lainie wondering what the fuck is wrong with me.

"So, Lainie, you got another job?"

She's sitting in my chair, typing away. I'm sitting in hers, watching.

"Another job?"

"Yeah, like, do you go to a job every day?"

Tapping her pretty chin with a pink-tipped finger, she responds, "Well, that's a difficult question to answer."

"How so?" This girl is somethin' else.

"While I don't have a job, technically, I've got my writing, as you know."

"Sure." I thought she said she was just getting started.

"And I've got a few irons in the fire elsewhere." She's not looking at me as she chatters about her irons. "But, no, I don't go to a job, per se."

Per se? "Do you want one? Temporarily? Until Molly gets back?"

She blinks her pretty eyes at me, adjusting a pair of glasses she pulled from somewhere up her nose a bit. Glasses are a good look for her. So good sexy librarian fantasies have started rolling around in my head. I wonder if she...?

"When will she get back? Is it full-time? What hours would I work? How much does it pay?" Pulling off the glasses, she looks at me with a stern expression. Like that sexy librarian telling me to *hush*. Fuck. And just like that, my cock is hard again. "And what about that kiss?"

Fuck. I'm in trouble. "What about the kiss?"

"We probably shouldn't keep kissing—"

"Why not? Why can't we work together *and* kiss?" Why can't we kiss? Or fuck? I lean forward in my seat, having come up with a genius idea. "Lainie. Think of it. If you worked here, some of the guys from the clubs will be in and out of here." Her finger taps her bottom lip again, and it makes me want to bite it. The lip, not the finger, although.... "Consider it research."

"Oh. Hm." She looks up at the ceiling like she's really ponderin' this shit. "Right."

"You could talk to them. Ask them questions for your story." With me in the room. I don't trust some of those bastards.

"That'd sure be nice." She's looking at me but not seeing me, lost in thought like she's too busy weighing her options. When her focus returns to me, a small smile slides across her lips. "Can I think about it?"

"Of course. Here." I pull out my wallet, extracting one of my cards. Searching Molly's desk for a pen, I find one under the debris. "Here's my cell," I say, jotting down my digits. "Call or text me tonight."

"Or tomorrow?"

"Sure, tomorrow works." Why can't she text me tonight? Is she going out? Does she have a date?

I watch her stand up from behind Molly's desk. Placing my card inside her purse, she slips the strap over her shoulder. "I'll call tomorrow."

"Or text. Either one." She moves toward the door. "Let me walk you out." I stand and place my palm on her lower back. It's the gentlemanly thing to do, right? She leads the way out of the office, down the corridor, into the showroom.

"This is impressive," Lainie says, looking back at me.

"Yeah?" I like that she's impressed. I've got some other impressive things I could show her.

She releases a giggle, and my dick starts up again. Jesus, I need to get laid. Preferably by a curvy little brunette I know. "You know it is. Eric said it's called Keeton's Brag Room."

Fucking Eric. "No, Eric calls it that because my little brother's a pain in the ass."

She stops walking, turning to face me, shock on her pretty face. "Little brother?"

"Yep. And Molly's my sister."

"So, this is a family business." It wasn't a question.

"It's mine, but I like having my family with me. They're all I've got."

"Oh," she says in a pitying voice. "I'm sorry."

"You've got family?" Why am I asking her this shit? I don't want to marry her. Fuck her, definitely. Marry her, no way. Never again.

"I've got four sisters who all live nearby, as well as my dad. My mom died when I was ten. Ovarian cancer."

Now it's my turn to sound pitying. "I'm sorry."

"Me too. I'm the lucky one. Since I was the oldest, I got to spend the most time with her." Sadness crosses her face and her eyes shimmer like she's going to cry, but she lifts her head, tossing it back a bit, and she's back to her happy self before I can blink an eye. Softly, she adds, "She was a wonderful mom. We were lucky to have her as long as we did."

She looks at me expectantly. I know what she wants. She wants to know about my folks. I can give her something, I guess. "My folks died when I was twenty-one."

"How?"

"Car accident."

She gasps. "Both of them? At once?"

"At once." I nod. I'm not going to tell her whose fault it was—that my dad couldn't stop drinking long enough to drive my mom home safely. The fucker.

"God, Keeton." She steps up to me and wraps her arms around my neck. Pressing her lush body against me, she whispers, "I'm so sorry."

It's my turn to hesitate, but not for long. I'm not passing up an opportunity to hold this girl. I wrap my arms around her and pull her to me. I can't help noticing how perfectly we fit together, like two puzzle pieces. I swear I can feel the beating of her heart against my chest. Not to be outdone, I whisper, "I'm sorry about your mom, too, baby."

She sniffles softly and says, barely audibly, "Me too, Keeton. Me too."

We stay like that for longer than we probably should. Long enough for Eric to walk in and open his damn mouth. "Well, that didn't take you long, brother."

Growling, I pat Lainie's bottom lightly and step away. "Eric, what can I do for you?"

"Just came to get you to sign off on this job. We're done."

"I'll be out in a few. I'm walking Lainie to her car."

"Is that what you call it?"

Lainie giggles again, and it sounds like tinkling bells. So fucking sweet, my girl. *My girl?* No. No way. I'm not going to do that to her. Sure, I was married once. Sure, it ended amicably, but every relationship since Deb has been a fucking train wreck. I suck at relationships. I should have just stuck it out with Debbie even though there was no spark there. None. The only thing we had in common was our love of machines. Hers? Muscle cars. Mine, bikes.

We walk in silence out to the piece of shit she's driving. "This your car?"

"It's my sister's."

"You don't have a car?"

"Nope." Opening the door, she tosses her purse in first. "Keely, my baby sister, lets me borrow it whenever I need it, so this is fine for now." Sliding in behind the wheel, she turns the key. Nothing. She tries it a second time, and the thing coughs to life. Barely.

I want to ask her why she doesn't have a car of her own. Didn't she get one out of the divorce settlement? But I keep my mouth shut. It's none of my damn business. "For now?" If she only has a car part of the time, how's she going to get here?

"For now. I'll go look for a used car sometime soon."

"I see." I probably shouldn't get involved, but this is my world. Besides, this old thing is spewing black smoke now. Oil leak. "I've got a good source for used cars. Reliable used cars," I say, looking down at the sad little Honda. Something on the fender catches my eye. Jesus. Is that duct tape? I feel compelled to pop the hood to make sure nothing else is taped together. I look at the front tire. Bald. This thing isn't safe enough for her.

"A good source?"

"Yeah." I walk to the front of the car. "Pop the hood, babe."

"It's fine, Keeton. She takes good care of it."

"This is what I do, Lainie. Pop the hood."

Releasing an exasperated sigh, she mutters, "Fine."

She reaches down for the latch and I hear the hood release and watch it as it pops up slightly. I press my fingers beneath the hood and lift. Finding the hood rod, I snap it into place. Peering down, I clench my jaw so hard it hurts. *Her sister takes good care of it? My ass.* Turning toward the garage I yell, "Eric! Bring me my tools."

"Be right out," he shouts back.

She's next to me now. Her hand is on my bicep. I flex it. I can't help it.

"Keeton, seriously. It's fine."

What's wrong with me? I can't seem to control that I'm feeling so fucking possessive over this girl. I turn to face her and place my palm on the back of her neck, like before. Leaning in, I kiss her lips softly. "Sweetheart, what kind of man would I be if I let you drive away in a car that's not safe? Huh?"

"Oh." She looks down at the engine. I know she can't see what I see, so I hope she trusts me. "It's not safe?"

"Baby, this is a death trap."

Her eyelashes are fluttering so fast, like a hummingbird. "It's not safe and my baby sister's been driving it?"

Now she's worried? But not about herself, for her sister? "That's right. It's not safe for her either."

"B-but can you fix it? Today? We need a car." She turns and starts to pace. "We can't be without a car. There's no bus service here. No Ubers. Nothing."

This rust bucket needs to get towed to the dump today, but I'm not sure she could handle that news right now. "Babe. It's okay."

Pacing more, she's now chewing on her fingernails. "Bicycles. The weather is nice now, not too hot yet. We could get some bicycles."

I stop her from pacing by blocking her current route. "Lainie? I've got an extra car." Or four. "I'll give you a loaner so we can take a look at this one." I point my thumb at the blue beater.

"No. I don't feel comfortable doing that. We just met."

"It's a *loaner*. Since you're going to be working for me for a while, I'll do all the repairs at cost and give you the loaner for free. I want you to get to work on time." I smirk, but she doesn't notice. She's seriously worried.

"At cost?"

I'm congratulating myself on sneaking that bit about her working for me past her, when she plants her hands on her hips and snaps, "Keeton. I haven't decided if I'm working here yet."

"Fine. But, take the loaner today. You can bring it back tomorrow after you've decided. How's that?"

"So, you're telling me Bessie's too dangerous to drive five miles?"

Bessie? "Yes." I look down at the engine again. "That's definitely what I'm saying."

Eric jogs up next to me and sets my toolbox down next to my feet. Stepping over to peer down under her hood, he whistles. "Jesus, babe. I can't believe this thing hasn't caught on fire yet."

Babe? I growl low in my throat. "Eric?"

"Yeah?"

He's oblivious. He throws around that word like it's nothing. Such a fucking player. Ignoring him, I turn back to Lainie. "So, yes? You take the loaner so Eric and I can take a look at your car?"

She's upset. So much so she snaps, "Fine. Thank you, Eric." She looks at me and her eyes soften, as does her voice. "And Keeton." Smiling at me. Just for me.

"No problem. Can't have my girl driving something that's not safe."

"My girl?" Eric says, laughing. "Shit, bro. You work fucking fast. I need to take some lessons."

"Fuck off, Eric. Grab her stuff out of that," I point at the blue beast, "while I drive the car around for her."

"Sure thing, boss."

CHAPTER FIVE

Lainie

I WATCH as Keeton appears from around the side of the building driving a sleek black sports car. A *new* sleek black sports car. "What the...?"

"Sweet ride, isn't it?" says Eric at my side. He's holding my purse as well as a sweater, umbrella, and a coat from the back seat.

"*That's* the loaner?"

"Loaner? Sure. If Keeton says so."

Something tells me that's *not* a loaner.

Keeton pulls up next to me, turning the car off before opening the door. "I can't drive *that*," I say, pointing at the five-million-dollar car.

"Sure, you can. It's an automatic. I wasn't sure if you could drive a manual."

"I can't drive a manual." I look at the car again and back to Keeton. "Can my sister drive it if she needs to?"

"Of course. No problem." Keeton's smiling. He looks sincere.

"Okay. Fine. But please don't fix anything on my car until you talk to me. If it's too expensive to fix, I'll have to talk to Keely."

"Who's Keely?" asks Eric.

"No one," grunts Keeton.

"My little sister."

"Sister, huh? Is she as hot as you?"

Is he kidding? I sputter for a second until I can think of a reply. "Keely's beautiful. She's sort of my exact opposite."

Both men stare at me for a second. "Baby," Keeton says, stepping closer to me. "You're the most beautiful girl I've ever laid eyes on. If your sister is the opposite, then she must be a real dog."

Eric chuckles. This entire conversation is confusing me. I pull my phone out of the pocket in my dress. Opening the photo app, I search for the picture of Keely from last summer. Her blonde hair is long and wavy around her shoulders. She's wearing a pretty white strapless sundress that shows off her perfect tan. It's my favorite picture of her. "Here." I hold out the image in front of the men. They'll see what I mean. They both stare at Keely, then at me.

"She's cute. That's for sure," says Eric. "But you're just as gorgeous, babe."

"Knock off with the *babe*, asshole," Keeton barks. He turns to me. "I stand by my previous statement, Lainie."

It takes me a minute to recall what his previous statement was. He's said a lot of things today. I'm the most beautiful girl he's ever seen? Impossible. "Okay, whatever." I shrug. I'm not going to get into a pissing match about who's prettier, me or my sister, because I already know. Keely's way prettier. I'm tempted to show them the rest of my sisters. They're prettier too. And I'm not saying that to get compliments. It's just a fact.

"Hop in. Call me later." He pauses. "Or tomorrow. Let me know what you decide."

I walk around the open car door and lean inside. I can smell the leather seats from here. The interior is black and sleek like the outside of the car. There are knobs and gadgets all over the dash. It's over-the-top fancy and luxurious. "What kind of car is this?"

"BMW," Keeton mumbles.

"It's a BMW M240i xDrive Coupe," Eric adds smugly.

I have no idea what he just said, but it sounds fancy and expensive. I'm tempted to look it up online, but then I think if I did, I'd never drive the car. "Oh. Wow. That sounds...."

Keeton chuckles. "It's just a car, Lainie. Hop in."

I slide onto the smooth leather and inhale. It smells like new car smell and him—musky and manly. I run my hands over the leather steering wheel and then let my right hand slide over the gear shift. I think I hear Keeton make a noise, but when I look over at him, he's silent. Just watching me admire his wheels, I guess. I look for the key but there's only a button. "Where do you put the key?"

Leaning down until he's a breath away, Keeton says, "No key. There's a fob in the cup holder. Put it in your purse. The car will unlock for you as soon as you touch the door handle. To start it, put your foot on the brake and press the button."

I do as he says, and it purrs to life. "Wow," I say with awe.

"You like it?" Keeton whispers close to my ear.

"It's amazing. Who wouldn't like it?" I've never driven a car like this. Lewis bought me a minivan. Ironic, since we were never going to have children. I think he thought it made him look like a family man if his wife had a van. Ugh, minivans.

This, whatever kind of car this is, is more my cup of tea. Someday, after my writing career takes off, I'll get something like this.

I turn back to Keeton. "You're sure?"

"Positive. Just promise me you'll stay within the speed limit."

"Of course."

"Once you hit the gas, you may change your mind." That's Eric talking from behind Keeton. "It's a turbo, so you'll be cruising, ba— I mean, Lainie."

"I'll be careful, guys. I promise." I can't make the same promise about my lead-foot sister, Keely. The girl is a menace on the road.

"Talk to you soon," Keeton says as he shuts my door,

I hear him tap the top of the car as I slide the gear shift into drive and hit the gas. Damn, the car jerks forward and out of the lot so fast I nearly lose control. Now I get what Eric meant by turbo. This thing is *fast*.

AFTER SPENDING over an hour with Keeton Gustafson, I drive away shaking my head. "What the heck just happened back there?" First I had to muster up the courage to walk into the shop, and then I practically had to talk myself into leaving. Now I'm driving the fanciest car I've ever seen. Owned by the hottest man I've ever met. It's like I was in some sort of trance at GCM. It's like that time my dad took us all to Graceland when I was fifteen. He loves Elvis. Anyway, I walked in not really liking his music. By the time we took the audio tour and stepped into the gift shop, I was hooked. It's like I was hypnotized—same as today.

Now that I'm a mile away, I can finally think straight. That man was intense. Sadly, there's no MC affiliated with his shop, but what I got was more interesting. I got kissed by a man who did it like it was his job and then said man offered me a job.

I feel like I need to debrief with my sisters. They'd listen to my tale and give me advice, a hug, or a fist bump if it was warranted. I think I need all three. I check the clock on the dash. Everyone should be done with work, classes, or whatever it is they're doing today. At a stop sign, I open my call app and hit my group number. It automatically dials everyone's number at the same time.

One by one, my four younger sisters start to answer. "Yo," says Keely, the baby—well, one of them. She and Violet are twins. Keely is a kindergarten teacher and by far the most tenacious one of the bunch. Never underestimate the youngest and smallest Palmer sister. Next is Sadie, the middle sister. She owns a little bakery in the town square called Sadie Cakes Bakery and sells the most delicious cupcakes imaginable. She makes other stuff, but cupcakes are my favorite, much to Lewis's chagrin. When she first opened the shop, he practically forbade me from going to visit. Yeah, like he could keep me from supporting my sister. Sisters before misters, am I right?

"Hey, girls," I say as we wait for the remaining siblings.

Agatha answers next, and Violet immediately after. Violet is so different from Keely, it isn't funny. Keely is short, about five-one, while Violet is the tallest sister, almost five-nine. Keely is petite, curvy, and compact. Violet, well, Violet isn't. Keely is outgoing and extroverted, and Violet is shy and introverted. Case in point, I know Violet is on the line because I see her number, but she's yet to speak. She's better one-on-one. Actually, Violet and I are close. I tell her just about everything because she's great at the advice thing, plus I know she'd take a secret to the grave. That's how loyal she is. I just wish she'd share some secrets with me. I know she has some.

Agatha speaks up. "Hey. What's up? I've only got a

minute." Agatha is a workaholic and two years younger than me. She's an accountant at a major shoe company. She works long hours trying to get the attention of a certain assistant human resources director at the same company so she can earn a promotion, among other reasons. She's tried several times, but she's always been passed over for a man. A man she most-likely trained. I continue to cross fingers for her, because my sweet Agatha deserves to be happy, and happiness for her means success at work.

It's strange—after all these years, I'm the only one who's married. Okay, who *was* married. Sadie is getting close. She's been dating her boyfriend, Andrew, for years. He's totally in love with her, so I'm sure he'll propose soon.

"Ladies, we need to powwow. I've got a story to tell you that involves a hunky motorcycle guy, a mad, passionate kiss, and a job offer."

"A mad, passionate kiss *and* a job offer?" snorts Keely. "Seriously? And by the way, that sounds an awful like a job doing the world's oldest profession. Am I right ladies?"

"Keely, *no*. Oh, my gosh. You are such a brat." Time to ignore that comment and get on with it. "As I was saying... You'll have to meet me for dinner if you want to hear the whole story."

"At Dad's or at Keely's?" asks one of my sisters. I can't tell which one.

Oh, that's a good question. I bet Dad would love to see us all at once. It's been a few weeks. "Dad's. We can eat, then go down to the family room to talk so he can't hear. I'll take care of the food."

"Okay. Gotta go," says Agatha. "See you there."

We all hear her phone click, and one by one the other three hang up too. I swing into the local grocery store to pick up several frozen pizzas and some salad mixes. Simple. Easy. Ordinarily, I'd prepare something delicious for my entire family, but there's no time. Frozen pizza is fine for tonight.

CHAPTER SIX

KEETON

"WELL?"

I look at my brother, who's still standing behind me. I'm watching the taillights of my new BMW glow off into the distance. "Well, what?"

"What the hell happened in the fifty-five minutes she was in your office? Is she pregnant yet?" He snorts.

"Jesus, Eric. You've got shit for brains, you know it?" Not really. The kid is whip-smart. He's just annoying. I step over to the little hunk of junk she drove here. Leaning down, I try to push the seat back, but I think it's rusted in that spot. "Come on, help me push this thing into the empty bay."

"I think we should just junk it and replace it with something better."

I arch my brow. "Oh yeah? You buyin' her a new car?" He'd better say no. If anyone's buying her a car, it's me.

"Nah, but I wouldn't mind buying her baby sis a car. That

chick was hot as sin."

"You said she was cute."

"Cute as in, I'd like to fuck her, cute." He pauses. "More than once."

Okay, that may sound really assholish, but for Eric, that's a compliment. He never sleeps with women more than once. "Don't even think about it. You'll upset Lainie if you mess with her sister, and I won't have you upsetting my girl."

"'My girl' again? You serious?"

Running my fingers through my short locks, I sigh. "I don't know. It's like she hypnotized me the second she walked into my office. I've never felt that way before. You know, smitten."

Eric cackles. "Smitten? Jesus, bro. What are you, a hundred?"

"Fine. Territorial. How's that? Like I didn't want anyone else to get near her. Ever. So, I'm thinking that makes her mine."

"Does she know?"

"She will," I mutter. "Now, come on. Let's push this thing inside. I need to get some shit done."

With Eric on one side and me on the other, we push the car into bay one. "Get Billy on this tomorrow, okay? I want a list of the shit that needs to be done to this thing. I'll decide where we go from there."

"Right on." I start to leave, but Eric grabs my arm. "She's a sweet girl, Keeton. You deserve some sweet in your life, bro."

I grunt. "We'll see."

"Hey," he yells just as I'm at the door to the showroom. "You need to sign off on this bike."

I turn. "Looks good. Call the broker. See if he's got time to come down to look at it." I work with a broker who sells the stuff that wasn't a commission. I don't like to deal with the hagglers and the nitpickers. We make 'em, he sells 'em. It works out great for all of us.

Back in my own office, I flop into my chair. Leaning back, I throw my feet on top of my desk and a stack of paperwork, muttering, "What the hell happened today?" I squeeze my eyes shut and lay my head back on my headrest. I need to wrap my head around this. It's not like me to just throw caution to the wind, especially when I'm dealing with a woman. I'm circumspect. It's why I've been successful—just the right amount of risk-to-caution ratio. But with this girl, that shit went out the window.

Reaching out, I hit the contacts on my phone, find the one I want, and hit call. After only one ring, she answers. "Hey, asshole. What's up?"

"Hey, Deb. Just thought I'd check in."

There's silence on the other end of the line. I know why. I don't check in with my ex-wife. I only call her when I've got a reason. Not because I don't like talking to her; on the contrary, I do. But we're both busy; we don't have time to chitchat.

"Like I said, what's up?" Yeah, see? She knows something's up.

"I'm having a weird day. Wanted to talk through it with you."

"Okaaaaay."

"Let me start at the beginning." So I do. I tell her about my first reaction to seeing Lainie at my door. About the hour I spent with her in my office. That I kissed her without giving it a second thought. When I'm done, I wait for her to speak.

See, here's the thing about Deb. She tells it like it is. She's a plain speaker. No bullshit. She doesn't have the time or the patience. The other thing—she's even less romantic than I am. She likes to fuck, and that's it. Deb never wanted flowers or candy or date nights, ever. Maybe that's why we didn't quite click. She and I are too much alike. And maybe I'd like a little bit of that romance shit. Just a little.

"Okay. Do you want me to be frank?"

"No. Lie to me."

"Ha ha."

"Yes. Say it."

"Okay. But, don't be pissed."

Shit. Why would I be pissed? "I won't be pissed." To her face.

"I love you. You know that, right?"

"I do." And I know she means she loves me like a friend or a brother. Yeah, we used to fuck, so the brother thing sounds creepy. Let's just go with *friend*.

"Keep in mind I've never met her, and you left out any description of her, but I'm going to tell you what I think she looks like first."

I wait.

"She's curvy and very pretty. Sweet, almost."

Shit. Does she have cameras in this place? I look around my office.

"Am I right so far?"

"Yes."

"I'm going to assume she's blonde, but that's not a deal-breaker."

"Brunette."

"Oh, interesting. She's around your age, maybe younger. She's feisty, but you know damn well she'd make you cookies if you're having a bad day and treat you like a fucking king."

Shit. "How?"

"She's naïve and a little shy."

"Fuck, Deb. How do you know this shit?"

She laughs. "Because she's my exact opposite."

"Shut the fuck up. Why would you say that?"

"Because I've known you for, what, twenty years? I know you loved me, but you, Keet, need someone who needs *you*. You want to take care of someone, and you want that person to take care of you too. I never needed you. I loved you, sure, but not that way. Does this woman need a man in her life, from what you could tell in an hour?"

"Not just any man." For fuck's sake. "She was married to a gay guy for ten years."

"Why? That's fucked-up."

"Not sure. I plan to get to the bottom of that." Bottom. Palmer-Bottoms. I also plan to get her to drop Bottoms as soon as possible. Maybe even add Gustafson to that hyphen. Holy shit, what am I saying?

"How could this happen this fast? You know how I am."

"When you know, you know. Yeah, that sounds fucking sickeningly romantic coming from me, but it's true. Some people never get that feeling you got today. I wouldn't discount it. Why don't you let yourself see where this goes? Don't hold back. This could be the icing on your cake, Keet. You've grown a successful business, you've taken care of your brother and sister, making sure they've got what they need. Now it's your turn. Icing. You can have it all. A woman who dotes on you and who gives you the family you've always wanted."

"I haven't—"

"*You have*. I swear you almost cried when you held Madalyn the first time. I know. I was there." Deb is one of my family. She's close to my sister and little brother. I got lucky with her. "I want to meet this girl. Do you think she'll take the job?"

"I hope so."

"Let me know. I'll drive down. We can get a beer or something after."

"Sure. Sounds good." I only hope Lainie takes the job. I want her here. Hell, I want her, period.

CHAPTER SEVEN

Lainie

WITH MY ENTIRE family assembled in my dad's dining room, I place two out of three pizzas in the center of the table, announcing, "Voilà, pizza is served."

I watch my dad scramble to his seat at the head of the table, and one by one my sisters follow. Back in the kitchen, I pick up the third pizza (sausage), and a fruit pizza I whipped up for dessert. By the time I make it back into the dining room, the pepperoni pizza is completely gone and the second is nearly there. "Geesh, people. Are you hungry or what?"

Mumbles and chewing sounds are all the response I get or need. I love to feed my family. "Save me a slice of that Hawaiian pizza, please." I didn't buy them like that. I bought basic cheese pizzas and doctored them up with our favorite toppings when I got here. Yeah, I know. When I add extra cheese and other goodies, I'm only adding calories. Lewis used to remind me of that on a daily basis. But that's what Mom used to do, so I do it too. *Suck it, Lewis.*

I snicker out loud, which causes all five to look up at me. "What?"

"You're laughing to yourself," Keely says. "Did you spit on our pizza or something?"

Violet giggles, while Sadie and Agatha look affronted. "No. Of course not. I just had a funny thought in my head. About Lewis."

A collective groan is heard from every member of my clan, my dad the loudest as he mutters, "Don't mention him at the table. I'll lose my appetite."

"Fine. Eat up. I made fruit pizza too." Placing that in front of my own spot, I slap away Keely's hand before she can take a slice. "Eat your dinner first, Keely."

She curses under her breath, muttering, "I'm not a baby. Jesus."

I know she's not a baby, but I have a hard time remembering that sometimes. "Sorry, Keels. I forget sometimes."

She reaches for the fruit pizza again, and I slap her hand away once more. My dad and remaining sisters laugh out loud.

"Assholes." That's Keely's only rebuttal.

I bite into the slice Violet sets on my plate and moan. "How can a frozen pizza taste this good?"

"Well, because once it got here, you made it something else," says Sadie. "You're good at that. Making something out of nothing."

I think about my marriage when she says that. I'm not sure why.

After dinner, Dad volunteers to clean up the dishes, what there are of them, while we make our way down to the basement. Agatha grabs a bottle of wine from the wine fridge, and Sadie brings five glasses.

"Okay, so what's this little meeting about?" That's Agatha.

"Well, I wanted to tell you all about my day at Gustafson Custom Motorcycles."

"Why did you go there?" Agatha again.

"Because she's writing a romance book about a biker gang and their bitches," Keely replies smugly.

"Seriously?" Sadie looks shocked. I guess I forgot to tell a couple of my sisters.

"Yes. I've been thinking about it for a while. I wanted to research it, you know, so I was writing from experience. Anyway, I scoped out this place and thought it was a motorcycle club. Guys in cuts were in there all the time."

"Cuts? What's that?" asks Violet.

"A cut is a leather vest. It usually has patches on it to tell us the name of their club."

"Okay, okay," says Keely, using her hand to motion for me to move along.

"I went over there to interview someone about the club. A super cute guy named Eric told me I had to talk to the boss. I followed him through the showroom, which was amazing by the way, down a long hallway to an office. The second I entered said office, I nearly fainted."

"Why?" asks Violet. She's moved to the edge of her seat, literally.

"Because," I sigh. "He was the most gorgeous man I've ever seen."

"What's his name?" Agatha asks, looking suspicious. I don't take offense. It's sort of her thing.

"Keeton Gustafson." I watch as she clicks around on her phone.

"Whoa. Is this him?" she says with awe.

I turn the phone to face me and nod. "That's him, only his hair is short now."

As she passes the phone around, I watch the reaction from each sister. It's unanimous. They all think he's hot too.

"Wait," says Keely. "On the phone today you said, and I quote, 'I've got a story to tell you about a hot biker dude, an inappropriate make-out session, and a blow job.' Right?" She blinks at me, then points at the phone. "You kissed this guy?"

My gosh, my little sister says the most outrageous things. "Well, I wouldn't say that. Definitely not about the b-blow job." I can barely say it let alone do it.

"Moving on..." Agatha huffs. "Why not? What did you mean by 'a mad, passionate kiss'?" Agatha says with air quotes.

"Because *I* didn't kiss him. *He* kissed me." Now, that little nuance may not be significant to you, but it is to me, and my sisters know that. They know everything—now. They didn't for a long time, however. They believed I was in a normal marriage, albeit an unhappy one. None of them liked Lewis even before Keely ran into him at one of the LGBTQ bars in Flagstaff. Afterwards, they hated him, assuming he was lying and cheating on me. I'll tell you more about the night the cat jumped out of the bag later. Right now, this is about me and my awesome day.

"So, he, what? Just grabbed you and kissed you?" Agatha thinks so analytically, I'm not surprised she doesn't get it yet.

I nod. "Yeah. I was just standing there." Standing there staring at his erection, but they don't need to know that. "He walked right up, put one hand on the back of my neck and the other one on my waist, and pulled me closer until I was right up against him. Then he kissed me, and it was like a kiss you read about in the best kind of romance. Hot." After my explanation, I wait for someone to say something, but they're all silent, staring at me. "What?"

"Did you kiss him back?" Violet asks shyly.

I blush. Even in front of my sisters. "I did."

They're all still staring at me. Finally, Sadie breaks the silence. Setting her wineglass down, she asks. "Start over. At the beginning. Tell us everything."

So, I do. I describe the scene like I'm writing about it—from the walk up to the building, to what I saw in the brag room, and then everything that happened in the office.

"Are you going to work for him?" Violet asks, her eyes as big as saucers.

"I don't know."

Clearing her throat, Agatha stands. "I'd like to say something."

I nod.

"You know I'm not very romantic and stuff, right?"

"Right," we all say in unison.

She scowls but continues. "I think you'd be doing yourself and your story a disservice if you didn't take that job. You deserve some hot, sexy romance, Lainie. Lewis was a manipulative jackass, something you didn't ask for when you agreed to marry that guy—to be his beard."

Since Keely discovered him all hot and heavy with his boyfriend at the club, they've all become very vocal about Lewis and my marriage.

I smile at Agatha. "Thanks, Aggie."

"Here, here," says Keely, raising her wineglass. She stares at Sadie, who hasn't moved. "I said, here, here."

Sadie points at her glass. "What? I'm empty. Fill 'er up."

Filling Sadie's glass, Keely continues, "Seriously, girl, you need to take that job and get all up on that man. He's going to rock your world."

"Keely, geesh," mumbles Violet. "You're sort of asking Lainie to be something she's not. You know, promiscuous."

Keely smirks. "Lainie's over thirty. She's no longer in 'trampy' territory. She's old enough to take what she wants because she wants it. No apologies, sis. None whatsoever." Once she's done, she sips from her glass like she just solved everything. "Oh, and where's my car?"

Oh, crap. "Well, that's another thing." I tell them what happened in the parking lot, about them taking Keely's vehicle and the loaner parked out at the curb in front of Dad's.

"*That's* the loaner?" Sadie nearly spits out her wine. "It's a BMW. I saw that and nearly wept. It's Andrew's dream car."

"The other one was a manual. So he gave me this one. I'm taking it back tomorrow; it's no big deal."

Violet looks at me, squinting like she's thinking really hard. "I think it's more."

We all stare at her. Like I said before, she rarely speaks, especially in a group setting.

"You do?"

"I do. You say he called you 'baby' and 'babe'?"

I nod.

"He kissed you several times out in the parking lot?"

"He did."

"Do you want my advice?"

We all say "yes" simultaneously.

"I'm with Agatha. You need to take that job and see what happens. There are too many what-ifs in this story. If you don't go back and see what it all means, you'll regret it for the rest of your life."

"You really think so?"

"I do. What if he's your person?"

Agatha gasps, Sadie makes a choking sound, and Keely giggles, adding, "Exactly."

My mom used to say Dad was her "person." That she knew the second she met him that she wanted him to be the father of her children. That he was the kind of man she'd always pictured herself with, strong but caring, tough but protective.

I think back to that moment I saw his picture and then the second I saw him in person, my heart beating so hard I feared it would jump out of my chest. I, in fact, *did* picture my children. The second his hand touched mine, there was a flash of my future children. It was instantaneous. I saw three of them. All blond. But as soon as he spoke, his deep, rumbling voice grabbed my attention. So much was going through my head that I hadn't stopped to consider that he might be my person.

CHAPTER EIGHT

KEETON

I FINALLY DRAG my tired ass home from the shop at eight. I spent the hour after Lainie left talking to Deb and then just thinking. About Lainie. Lainie and me. Nothing was resolved in my head. How could it be? I've never in my life acted so spontaneously with a woman. I take that back; I've picked women up at bars whenever the need arose, but booze-induced hookups don't count.

Pulling into my garage on one of my bikes, I park, turn off the engine, and look around at the four-car garage attached to my new home. My new home on three acres of land. My new home with four bedrooms, six baths, and a gourmet kitchen. I designed it myself and it wasn't until this precise moment that I understand why I designed the house like this. It's because I want to fill it up. Fill it up with a family. I swear to fuck I didn't know I was doing it. Both Eric and Molly scratched their heads at each revision to the design I created. It kept getting bigger and bigger. More bedrooms one time, a game room in the basement the next. A pool in the backyard surrounded by an iron safety fence was the final addition before I signed off on it, handing it over to the architect who would get it ready for the builder.

I gulp as I run my hand through my hair. The realization that this is what I've been waiting for—Lainie is what I've been waiting for—is daunting. I feel my eyes burn. There's no fucking way I'm going to cry, right? I'm a thirty-fucking-six-year-old man. I don't cry. I feel wetness on my cheek and I wipe it away quickly. I must have dirt in my eye.

Shaking it off, I slide off my bike and walk through the door to my home, into my kitchen. "I need a damn beer." Maybe I should call one of my hookups. You know, to get this shit out of my system. To get Lainie out of my head. I shouldn't want this, her. I'm happy, right?

Deb's words float around me. *Now it's your turn. Icing. You can have it all. A woman who dotes on you and who gives you the family you've always wanted.*

It's fucking uncanny. I know Deb's right. Lainie would be the sweetest thing I've ever had in my life. I'd treat her like a fucking queen. A goddess. And just like I know what I'd do, I'm positive she'd do the same for me and our kids. "Fuck!" I shout into my cavernous, empty house. *House.* Not home. Not yet.

I stomp out of the kitchen, through the great room, down the hallway to my bedroom. Stripping down, I walk into the bathroom and turn on the steam shower. I need to relax. Drink my beer and watch some hockey or something. The Vegas Golden Knights should be on; I'll focus on that.

I don't linger in the shower. I'll jack off if I spend too much time there. I'm out in five minutes, and in a tee and clean boxer briefs in five more. I lie on my bed and flip channels on the television on the wall. Finding something entertaining to watch takes me a few. As I scroll through the channels, I hear my phone chime. Probably Molly. I didn't check in with her today.

Sliding off my bed, I walk to my dresser and grab my phone. I don't recognize the number.

Unknown Number: *Hi, Keeton. This is Lainie Palmer-Bottoms. You know, from earlier today?*

Fuck yes. My heart starts to pound in my chest. It's a foreign feeling for me. Nothing shakes me like this girl. Nothing.

Me*: Hey, beautiful.*

I wait for her to respond. It takes her too long. What happened? Moving back over to my bed, I mute the television so I can focus on her. While I wait, I add her name to my contacts: My Lainie.

What? Don't be shocked. This girl is *mine*.

Me*: You still there?*
My Lainie*: Oh, yes. Sorry. I'm here.*
Me: *What are you doing tonight?*

I'm dying to ask her what she's wearing but I don't think I should go there. Yet.

My Lainie*: I just got home.*

Just got home? Where's she been? Out? If so, with whom?

Me*: Just got home?*

I look at the clock.

Me: *It's late, baby.*

I wait for a response, but she's taking her sweet time.

My Lainie: *Why do you keep calling me that?*
Me: *Calling you what? Baby?*
My Lainie: *Yes.*

The answer to that question is more complicated than I can cover in a text, so I simplify it.

Me: *It feels right.*
My Lainie: *Oh.*
Me: *Why are you getting home so late?*
My Lainie: *I was at my dad's. My sisters were there. We had dinner together.*

Shit. Did she talk about me? I'm fucking dying to know. No. I did not just think that. It's official. I surrender my man card.

Me: *Good time?*
My Lainie: *Very. My family is awesome. ;)*
Me: *I'd like to meet them sometime.*

Oh, shit. I did not just say that.

My Lainie: *Really? Why?*
Me: *Because they're your family. I want you to meet Molly and Madalyn.*
My Lainie: *That's her baby's name? I love that name.*
Me: *Yep. Baby Maddy. She's gorgeous just like her mama. Hang on, I'll send you a picture.*

I search my photos to find a picture of me holding the baby the day she was born.

My Lainie: OMG! She's so cute. You look good holding her too.

Fuck yes.

Me: I'm a natural. ;) The ladies love me.
My Lainie: LOL
Me: What? You don't agree? You wound me.
My Lainie: Oh, no. I didn't mean to laugh at that. I thought you were just being funny. I'm so sorry, Keeton. I didn't mean to hurt your feelings.
My Lainie: Shoot. I should go. Have a good night.
Me: NO! Fuck, I WAS kidding. It's hard to tell when you're texting. Can I call you? Then you'll hear my voice and know when I'm teasing.
My Lainie: ...
Me: Please?

I'm fucking begging now. It's over. I'm officially pussy-whipped and I haven't even gotten a taste yet. She doesn't respond. I'm nearly beside myself when my phone vibrates in my hand. "Hello?"

"Hi, Keeton."

"Lainie," I say almost breathlessly. "Thanks for calling."

She laughs softly. A tinkling laugh. "Sure thing."

"So, are you calling to tell me you'll help me out at the shop?"

"Um, yes. I'll help you. When do you want me to start?"

"Tomorrow, first thing, if you can."

"I can, but, uh, I can't work the entire day tomorrow. I'll

need to leave at three. Actually, my hours will need to be flexible in general, if that's okay."

"That's fine. You can just jot down your hours somewhere. I'm flexible."

"Okay."

There's a pause on her end of the line. I know she wants to ask me something else. "What else, angel? What else do you want to ask?"

"How—how much does it pay?"

My girl's worried about money? Didn't that fucking ex of hers leave her set? I grit my teeth. I don't even know him or the story, but I still want to fuck him up. "How's thirty an hour?"

"Thirty dollars?" she says, sounding shocked, squeaky.

"Not enough? Forty?"

"Oh my gosh, Keeton. I was thinking ten." She giggles. "Thirty is insane."

"It's what I pay Molly." Yeah, she's my sister, so I pay her well.

"Well, I've never been an office manager before, Keeton. I don't deserve the same pay as Molly."

She thinks she doesn't deserve to get paid? God, I want to take this woman, wrap her up in my arms, and tell her how much she deserves. So much. She deserves everything. I know she does. "Lainie. The job pays thirty. Don't argue with me."

"Oh." She sounds surprised. "I'm sorry. Okay."

Fuck. Now she's just being obedient. In the bedroom, that's a plus; in normal life, not so much. "Lainie, sweetheart," I say softly. "I didn't mean to sound so harsh. The job is not easy. I'm a terrible boss. I'm disorganized, forgetful, and an asshole most days. You're going to wish you took the forty by the time you're done."

She laughs. "Okay, Keeton. If you say so."

I say so, but I don't say it out loud. I get the feeling I'll need to treat my woman with kid gloves until she understands what's happening here. In the meantime, I need to know more about her fucking ex. "Good. Now, tell me about your ex-husband."

"What?" she squeaks again. "Why?"

"Call it curiosity."

"Keeton...."

"Tell me, honey. I need to understand it. You knew he was gay when you married him. Why did you do it?"

CHAPTER NINE

Lainie

HIS QUESTION IS JUST FLOATING out there in space. *Tell me, honey. I need to understand it. You knew he was gay when you married him. Why did you do it?* I can't figure out why he wants to know. Not only that, I'm not sure I'm prepared to tell him.

"Lainie?"

Kicking off my shoes, I lie down on my bed. "I married him because he asked."

"Is that all it takes to get you to marry someone? If that's the case...."

"No." I laugh. "I was nineteen, almost twenty. I'd never had a boyfriend. I was always the third wheel."

"The third wheel," he repeats, but it's not a question.

"Yes. Years of being the poor, fat, single girl was enough for me. So, when Lewis told me he needed cover for him to achieve his career goals, I agreed."

"You're not fat, babe. You're curvy and lush. Damn, it's making me hard again just thinking about you."

I ignore him, because I need to keep going. If he wants to hear this, I need to do it now. "Anyway, it helped us both out, so I said yes. We married a few weeks later at the courthouse."

"No big wedding?"

"No."

"Did you want one?"

God, why is he asking me this? "Keeton, *every* girl wants a big wedding. But it would have been a lie. Besides, I couldn't do that to my dad. Weddings are expensive."

"I get that." He sighs on the other end. Is he frustrated with me? "What happened after you got married? Did you buy a home together? A car? Did you go to college?"

"We moved into his condo. We lived there the entire time. We each had our own bedroom. We had one car for the first two years, then he bought me a used minivan."

"A minivan? Did you have children?"

"No. He wanted to give the appearance he was a family man. He works at the bank. He had career aspirations. I was part of his scheme to earn promotions. The little woman at home, you know?"

"Why don't you have a car now?"

I don't know why I'm telling him any of this. He seems to care about me, and for some reason, I feel the same about him. "Everything was in his name. I signed the divorce papers on the spot. I didn't even have my own attorney. By the time I was served, I just wanted out."

"Fuck," he spits. "What kind of settlement did he give you?"

"None."

"None!" he shouts. "You provided him cover for ten years so he could make a name for himself at work and you got nothing?"

"I had an allowance."

"I've never wanted to pummel someone as much as I do your ex-husband. Why the fuck do you still use his name?"

"I'm used to it."

"That's it? You're used to it? Jesus, woman."

Okay, I've had enough. He's starting to sound like Lewis. His tone is getting accusatory. I'm not doing that again. "I've got to go." I hang up the phone without another thought. I let the tears roll down my cheeks the same way. Crying is cathartic, and I need something cathartic.

Keeton: *I'm sorry. I know how I sounded. Like an asshole. What you call yourself is your business. I overstepped. Forgive me?*

That's something I'm not used to. Apologies. Lewis never apologized. Ever. I wait a few minutes before I respond.

Me: *Apology accepted. See you tomorrow.*

I'll have to show Keeton that I'm not going to put up with another Lewis. No way. He's right about my name though. It's why I have to leave early tomorrow—I'm going to the courthouse to officially change my name back to Palmer. And that decision was mine, and mine alone. No man told me to do it. There were a few women, four to be exact, encouraging me to change it, but that's different. They're my sisters.

CHAPTER TEN

KEETON

I FORGOT to tell Lainie what time to be at work, so when I pull into the lot on my 1948 Indian Chief motorcycle, I'm surprised to see her. Happily surprised. I roll up next to her sitting in my Beamer, and she slides the window down. Smiling down at her, I say, "You made it."

"I did. You didn't tell me when to start, so I just went by the business hours listed on your website."

"Smart." I wink. "Follow me. We'll park in the back."

I pull up far enough for her car to circle around and lead her to the back lot, watching her in my side mirror. She looks really pretty today. I don't even know what she's wearing yet, but I already know she's beautiful.

Once we're parked, I slide off my bike and watch her step out of the car. I'm not disappointed. She looks like she's going to work in the *Mad Men* ad office in her tight black skirt. It hits her right below her knees. I look down first and see she's got on a pair of black spiked heels. They cap off her gorgeous legs perfectly. My eyes follow the line of her hip, past the dip in her waist to her blouse. It's white, with a little rounded collar and those same puffy sleeves as yesterday. It's a little snug, the buttons pulling right near her breasts. I'd love to see what she's got on underneath that top, but my eyes finally meet hers. She's smirking. "Like what you see?"

I throw my head back and laugh. She tossed what I said to her yesterday back in my face. "I do. I like it very much. You look good enough to eat." I growl the last part. Her face flushes. I should feel bad about that, but I don't. Pink is so pretty on her.

Stepping closer to me, she touches the saddlebag of my classic bike. "This is beautiful." Her finger runs over the soft leather of the seat to the red of the gas tank, and up to the bars. Her nails are still pink and short, like she nibbles on them. A nervous habit, no doubt.

"It's my dream bike. I've wanted it ever since I could remember. I finally bought it last year from a guy in Phoenix."

"I can see why you love it. It's regal."

Regal. That's the perfect word to describe my Chief. "It is that. I'll take you for a ride someday." I nod down to her skirt. "You'll want to wear jeans, though. Not that I wouldn't like to see you on the back of my bike in that skirt hiked up to your hips. I just don't want any other assholes getting a peek." *Because you're mine, Lainie.* "Come on. Let's get inside." I walk to the back door and pull out my keys. "I'll make you a key in case you get here before me."

"Oh, are you sure?"

"Positive. Let me show you how to turn this place on." I lead her to a utility closet that houses one of our furnace and air-conditioning units. "The breaker box is in here. Just flip this main lever here and everything turns on. If Eric gets here before you, he may have already turned this on so, don't freak out if my bike's not here and the lights are on."

She nods. "Sounds good."

I step out of the doorway and lead her out to the main room. "There's one more switch here." I point to the toggle on the wall. "This switch lights up the display cases and the neon signs."

"Oh, I didn't notice those before."

I've got two neon signs in the space. One is the classic Indian Motorcycle ad sign of the Chief's head and the Indian name. The other is a newer Harley Davidson winged bar and shield sign Eric bought me for my birthday a couple years ago.

"I like the neon. It gives the place a sort of vintage vibe."

"That's what I was going for." She gets it.

She turns to face me. "Well, you did it."

Her smile is almost as pretty as the one yesterday. Almost. The one yesterday changed my life. I chuckle at myself. I'm about to speak, but the phone rings. "Damn it," I mutter.

"I'll get it."

I watch her run down the hall the best she can in that tight skirt and high heels. It's something I'd like to see every day in these hallways.

From my spot I hear her. "GCM, this is Lainie, how can I help you?"

I step closer to eavesdrop. In case she has questions.

"Oh. How did you...?" She pauses, listening to whoever is on the other end. Her voice sounds shaky.

I lean further into the room so I can really listen.

"Well, I'm just temping. Molly, the office manager, is out on —" She pauses again.

Who the hell is she talking to? The only thing I can gather from this side is that the caller is an asshole.

"I'm sorry? No. I—"

I step into the office. I don't like the way she sounds—upset. Well, fuck that. I can't let her deal with an angry customer on her first day of the job. I walk over to her and reach for the receiver, whispering, "Lainie. Let me."

She releases it, looking back at me. Her face is flushed again, but not in a good way. Her eyes are watery. What the ever-loving fuck?

"This is Keeton."

A man says, "Who the fuck are you? I was talking to my *wife*."

Her ex-husband is calling her at work? "Ex-wife, you mean?"

"I asked you a question. Who. The. Fuck. Is. This?" The douche is belligerent, that's for sure.

I'm not going to stoke this asshole's flame. Not when I look over at Lainie and see her biting her pink nail. So, I calmly say, "Keeton Gustafson."

"Well, Keeton Gustafson," he spits, "put my fucking wife back on the line unless you're the one she's whoring around with. Did you buy her that car?"

I pull the phone away from my ear, lean down, and hang it up. No need to listen to that shit anymore.

Lainie is still visibly upset. "I'm sorry, Keeton. I didn't tell him. He—"

"He must have seen you or heard something. This is a small town, babe."

"I'm so sorry, Keeton. Let me call one of my sisters to come get me. I don't want you to have to deal with that at your place of business." She picks up her purse and starts to step around me.

I quickly wrap my arms around her and pull her to me. She's looking everywhere but at me. "Look at me, honey." She shakes her head, so I place my finger under her chin and gently urge her to face me. Her eyes are shiny with tears. "That wasn't your fault. That's on him. He's the one that interrupted *you* at work. He's the asshole here. Besides," I swipe my finger over her pretty plump cheek, "I need for you to stay and help me out, Lainie. I'm in over my head with this bookkeeping shit."

She laughs even though she's distressed. "True. You are in over your head."

"I am. I need you by my side." Every day.

Blinking, she looks up at me. "How did he know I was here?"

That's a good question. "Would he follow you?"

"No. Why would he?" She pauses. "I didn't notice anyone behind me on my way here."

He could be tracking her phone. Oldest trick in the book. "Did he give you your phone?"

She looks down at her hand; the one holding her iPhone. "Yes. It's the only thing he let me keep. He said he'd pay my bill for a year." She looks at me again. "Why didn't he just call my phone?"

"Who knows? Probably letting you know he knows where you are right now." Nodding to her phone, I ask, "May I see it?" She hands it to me, and I search her apps. Flipping through her home screens, I come across one I recognize. I wonder if she does. "What's this one?" I ask, pointing to the icon.

"I don't know. I think it was there when I got the phone."

I hit the app and see a log-in screen appear. "You didn't log in to this?"

"No. Why?"

I pull my own phone out and do a quick search, bringing up the site that explains what she's got on her phone. I hand it to her.

Scanning the page I found, she gasps. "Oh, my God, Keeton. This tracks my location, my text messages, and my

Facebook page?" Reading a bit more, her eyes double in size. "This thing can see my pictures and videos?" She looks up at me. "It can even track what I'm searching for on the web." Her face morphs from fear and sadness to anger in seconds. "Are you trying to tell me that that weasel has been reading my text messages? Looking at my photos?"

I shrug. "I don't know. When did he give you this phone?"

"About a week before I was served papers."

"Could be a coincidence."

"What are you saying?"

"I'm not saying anything except your ex-husband could be monitoring you through your phone."

"But why?"

"Who knows? Is he the jealous type?"

"How could he be jealous? He's gay."

"I can't answer that question. Maybe if you told me more about him, about the two of you, I can help you figure this out."

Her eyes grow round. "Do you think it was on my old phone too?"

"Maybe."

"I've still got it. The old phone. In a box somewhere. When I get home tonight, I'll find it and charge it up."

"Let's assume he's been monitoring you for a while. I don't think you should alert him to the fact that you know. Not yet. Maybe we could play with him a little bit."

She shakes her head slightly. "I'll never be able to trick him. I'm not devious like that."

"Leave that to me. I'm devious enough for the both of us." Still in my arms, I watch Lainie work through all of this. I can almost see the cogs spinning in her pretty head. I run my palm up the center of her back and down slowly. Repeat. Her breathing seems to return to normal in minutes. I gently nudge her closer to me. "Sweetheart?"

That gets her attention, "Huh?" She blinks up at me.

I lean down and kiss her full lips. Just a soft kiss. Not the kind of kiss I really want to give her. She leans into the kiss, which I decide is a good sign. "Don't worry. We'll figure it out. Together. Okay?"

"Right. Okay." Pulling away from me, she sits behind Molly's desk. "We'd better get to work, huh? You're not overpaying me to sit around gabbing all day."

"Right," I chuckle. "Get to work, babe."

CHAPTER ELEVEN

Lainie

WHERE DO I start with everything that happened this morning? First of all, what the heck was up with Lewis and that terrible phone call? Could he really be tracking me with that app? After Keeton went to his office, I read more about it. It's certainly invasive. It's designed for parents to watch over their children, not for husbands to spy on their wives, or in this case, ex-wives. Could he have been doing that through our entire marriage? I had my previous phone for two years. I lean back in my chair, closing my eyes, trying to think back to the times Lewis knew something about me that he shouldn't; like if he referenced something about someone I was texting or who I went to lunch with. I shake my head, unable to think straight.

I sit up suddenly. It hits me. He always seemed to bump into me when I was out for lunch with one of my sisters or a friend. We do live in a small town, but it wasn't just here. I recall a few times in Flagstaff. Heck, one day he was just walking past my doctor's office as I exited after a checkup. We'd always laugh it off as a coincidence, but was it? "What the ever-loving heck?"

Time for a group text. Oh, wait. I can't send a text. What if Lewis really is monitoring my phone? Instead, I open up my email account on Molly's computer. I pause. How am I going to word this question?

> From: Lainie Palmer-Bottoms
> To: The Palmer Sisters
>
> Hey girls. Listen up. I've got a super serious question for you all. You're going to have to think back a couple of years. Here's the question: Do any of you recall Lewis either a) showing up places out of the blue, seemingly like a coincidence, or b) knowing something about you, me, any of us that he shouldn't have known? I'll explain why I'm asking you tonight. Meet at Murphy's for wings at 7? You can tell me if you remember anything like that then. <3 Lainie

I close the email account and return to my work, which hasn't been too terrible so far. I've only had to ask Keeton one or two questions related to his computer system. Either Keeton didn't mess this up as badly as he thought, or he hadn't been at it long enough. I get how to search for invoices, I can do the books, and I can file, of course. The part of this job that requires Keeton's help revolves around the invoices and names of parts. I mean, what the heck is a camshaft? And don't get me started on the Evo Motor Carb Ignition. Huh? What? So, yeah, those are the kinds of things that Keeton needs to explain to me. And also, if we've received the items on the purchase orders so I can pay the bills.

I'm hip-deep in paperwork that afternoon when Keeton shows up at my office door holding up a brown bag and announcing, "Lunch is served."

I blink up at him in surprise. Then I just stare. The man is unbelievably good-looking. Not only that, just having him within five feet of me is causing my internal lady bits to go haywire. *Get it together, Lainie.* "Lunch?" Wow, the morning flew by. "You bought me lunch?"

"I did." He says, beaming.

Even though I have my lunch in my oversized purse, I keep quiet about it. "Thank you. That's very sweet." This could be a working lunch—a great opportunity to go over the orders with him.

"Follow me. Let's eat in my office."

I stand, picking up the papers that I need to ask him about, and follow him out of Molly's office. We take a right down the hall and then a quick left. I step into the inner sanctum of GCM, watching as Keeton holds a chair out for me at a small round table that sits in the middle of his office. "Thank you, kind sir." I giggle like the dork I am.

"So." He sighs. "I wasn't sure what kind of lunch you preferred. I've brought you several choices."

"Alright." Whatever it is, it smells amazing.

Opening the first bag, he pulls out a plastic container. "This one is chicken tenders and fries."

Oh, I love those. But I'd better not. Too many calories.

"This one," he holds up another container, "is a club sandwich and potato chips."

That's good too. I could just eat the sandwich filling without bread and skip the chips. I raise my hand like I'm about to reach for that one when he pulls out yet another container.

"Cheeseburger and fries."

Wow, the charbroiled smell is wafting into the room. It smells delicious.

"And lastly, I've got some mac and cheese. What's your poison, beautiful?"

I'd love to tell him all of them, but really, I shouldn't eat any of it. Nothing he has is less than a thousand calories. I'm sure of it. "Well," I say hesitantly. "Um...."

I look up and see his blond brows furrowed. He's worried. "Shit, babe. You don't like any of these, do you? I should have asked. I just wanted to surprise you. What do you want? I'll run back out and get it."

"No. I. Oh, shoot, Keeton." Oh, heck. I can't tell him I'm not going to eat his choices. "I like them all, it's just...."

"What?"

I'm on a diet. I brought a salad. But I can't bring myself to say it. He's so dang sweet to buy me lunch. Smiling, I tap my bottom lip like I'm trying to decide. "I like it all. I just can't decide."

The relief that crosses that gorgeous man's face is priceless. "Shit. You scared me for a second. You can have it all. I'll just eat what you don't."

"No. Don't be silly. May I please have the club sandwich?" I'll just skip the chips. Most of them, anyway.

"You really like everything I picked?" His chest has puffed out, shoulders back. He's so proud of himself.

"I do. It's like you read my mind." I giggle. I really do love everything. Too much, unfortunately. It's my love of food just like this that gave me this pudgy body.

"Let's eat." He sits across from me, opening up the cheeseburger and fries. Taking a huge bite, chews, then nods toward the stack of papers as he swallows his food. "You got questions for me?"

I'm about to take a small bite of my sandwich, but I set it back down. "Yes. I need to know if you've received these parts." I add, mumbling, "Whatever they are."

He laughs. "Funny names, right?"

"Yes!" I say excitedly. He gets it. I lean down to read the top invoice. "What the heck is a crankcase?"

"Well," he says, wiping off his hands, "a crankcase is the housing for the crankshaft in a reciprocating internal combustion engine."

What the heck? It makes absolutely no sense. "Oh." I shrug, taking a bite of my sandwich. "Of course."

Keeton releases a low, rumbly laugh that makes me feel tingly again. "You're so fucking adorable, Lainie. I just want to wrap you up and take you home."

"Oh?" I squeak. I feel the heat of my blush run up to my cheeks in milliseconds. The truth is, I want him to take me home. But instead of wrapping me up, I want him to *un*wrap me. My face must give me away, because Keeton's eyes grow dark and hooded. Sultry.

"You like the sound of that, Lainie?" he asks, all growly. "You want me to take you home?"

Yes. "Um...." Yes.

Keeton stands up, dropping his napkin down on top of his half-eaten burger. Stepping over to his door, he pushes it shut and flips the lock. Uh-oh. A shiver runs through me, but it's not out of fear. It's because I'm suddenly turned on more than I've ever been. I've never wanted anyone more than I want Keeton.

As he stalks back to me, I stand, turning toward him. I'm not afraid. I want this. Before I can take another breath, Keeton's hands are all over me. In my hair, sliding over my back to my big derriere. When he presses me to him, I feel his hard length up against me. "Lainie, I swear to fuck, I've never wanted any woman more than I want you. If you don't want this, me, speak now. Because there's no turning back once I have you. After that, you're fucking mine. You get me?"

This is not happening. It can't be real. So, if it's not real, why don't I just play along? I nod frantically. I want him to shut up and kiss me, but words aren't my forte right now. His mouth is on mine before I can take another breath. I'm meeting him in the middle. Our tongues are moving against each other's. Next, his mouth moves over mine, sucking on my top lip, biting on my bottom one. It's intense. I feel so charged, I wrap my arms around him and slide my own hand onto his bottom. "Oh, God." His ass is so hard and round; it's the bottom of my dreams.

Keeton moans right against my ear as he slides his tongue and teeth down the column of my neck. I think I could orgasm just from this. Pulling one hand from his bottom, I slide it forward, skimming the back of my hand up his hardness.

"Fuck, woman. That's it!" He sounds angry, but I think it's something else, since he's got both of his hands on my butt, lifting me off the ground. I squeal in shock. I've no time to stop him, warn him he's going to throw his back out, because I feel myself being set down on a hard surface. His desk. I watch as he slides his hands up the inside of my skirt, pushing it up. "Lift that ass up a little, baby. Let me get to that pussy."

Oh, geesh. Dirty talk. I've never.... But I wish I had.

"Now, honey. Now," he says urgently.

I use my hands as leverage to lift my butt off the desk while Keeton pushes my skirt up over my hips. It's then I remember which underwear I've got on. Haines Her Way briefs. Pink. Not even the high leg ones. I cringe inwardly, but he doesn't seem to care. "Up. Lift up," he says frantically. I do it again as he slides my big panties down past my hips, over my knees and shoes and off. "Fucking finally," he sighs.

He's staring at the juncture of my legs, since I've closed them tightly. Panting, he moves his hands slowly up my legs, between my thighs, putting some pressure on me. "Open your gorgeous legs for me, honey. Show me."

When I don't move, he looks up at me. Our eyes meet. "Baby," he whispers. "Open your legs. Show me. If you don't want anything else today, I'll stop, but I need to see."

His eyes have gentled. There's still fire in them but I believe him. I barely nod as I slowly open my legs. I've no idea what's going on down there. It's a jungle, I know that. I've never done the waxing and stuff like Keely does. Now, I wish I had. But it is what it is. I feel his palms again on the inside of my legs; he's helping me open wider. Such a gentleman, I think to myself, which makes me giggle since this is *so* not gentlemanly.

"You nervous, Lainie?"

"Definitely." Because I am.

Once my legs are wide enough, he stares down. "Tell me I'm the only one, Lain."

"You're the only one," I croak.

Jerking his head up, he stares at me. "Say it again. Use my name."

"You're the only one, Keeton."

He looks down at me again. I should probably feel self-conscious, but the way he's looking at me is intense.

"Well," he says, running his hands back down my thighs. He stops at my knees. With gentle pressure, he pushes my legs back together. "That changes things."

What? It changes things? Just because I'm a virgin, for all intents and purposes, now he doesn't want me? I guess he saw me and it disgusted him. Why else would he push my legs back together? I quickly start to slide off the desk. I feel the burn of tears, but I will not cry. This is par for the Lainie Palmer course. I'm used to this. It happened in high school on my one and only date. Tod Mendenhall touched my stomach, then told me I was too fat to screw. The difference between then and now? Nothing. It still hurts the same. The same humiliation is coursing through my body that I felt when I was sixteen.

Pushing my skirt down as I go, I land on my high heels and wobble a little. Keeton steadies me, but I slap his hands away. Yes, you heard me. I slapped them away. Without another word, I try to move past him, but he's bigger than me, if you can believe that. He's blocking me. "Move, Keeton," I say angrily.

"Baby, stop."

"Do *not* call me baby." I push on his chest, but he doesn't budge.

"Lainie. I said that wrong."

"You think?" My voice wavers, and I literally bite my tongue to stop any tears from escaping. Focus on the pain, because he doesn't get my tears.

I push again, but this time, he wraps his big arms around me, lifting me off the ground. "Put me down. I'm going to hurt you."

I feel his hand reach down beneath my legs so now he's holding me like a child. I kick out, but it's no use. "Honey, please stop. Let me start over. You misunderstood."

I won't look at him. I can't.

Walking over to a long leather sofa, he sits down with me on his lap. His grip is firm so I'm unable to squirm away.

"I meant that it changed how I approach this with you. If I'm your first, honey, it needs to be special, romantic. Not on my desk in my office. We can do that next week, I promise. The first time for us shouldn't be fucking on the office furniture. No, the first time we make love, it will be in my bed."

I'm still not looking at him. But I'm listening.

"I want to do this right. Take you out on a date."

"You want to court me?" Now I look at him.

"If that's what you want, I'll court the fuck out of you, sweetheart."

That makes me laugh. Only Keeton Gustafson could make courting sound dirty.

"Not a long courtship. Maybe one night?" I say shyly.

"Thank fuck. If you made me wait for months, my dick might fall off."

"I was willing to do it today," I say, arching one brow.

"And I appreciate that. But I want this with you. Do you? Want it with me?"

"Sex? Yes." I laugh. "Yes. For some crazy reason, I do. Even though we just met, it feels like I've known you forever."

"I know." He runs his palm down my leg, then kisses my nose. "I know, baby." He nudges me off his lap until I'm standing. Pulling himself up to stand next to me, he adds, "So, be ready by seven."

"Oh, I can't tonight." Here we go. I'm going to tell him I'm going out with my sisters, and he's going to launch into a rant about spending too much time with my family and not enough time with him. Lewis always did.

"You can't?"

"No. I can't tonight. I'm going out with my sisters."

"Oh, all right. Tomorrow?"

What? That didn't just happen. "Sure. Tomorrow." He's not upset? He doesn't ask me to cancel my plans with them? What's happening?

"Wear something sexy, I'm taking you somewhere fancy."

"No. I don't need fancy." That's all we ever did when Lewis and I went out. I'm sick of fancy. "Let's go somewhere on your motorcycle."

He looks shocked. His eyebrows are halfway up to his hairline. "Really? You want to ride on the back of my bike?" He pulls me to him again.

"What?" Is he upset about that? "We don't have to."

"Only my old lady rides on the back of my bike."

"Right. I'm sorry. I didn't realize." I thought he said he didn't have an old lady. Once again, I've misunderstood the rules of the game. When will I ever learn?

"If you get on the back of my bike, Lainie, it's official."

"Official?"

"My very own old lady."

"Really? Are you serious?"

"As the dead."

"All right then. I'll wear jeans."

"Good. Pick you up at seven. Bring a jacket."

"Okay. I'll be ready."

"Text me your address later." He pats my bottom. "I need to get back to work. And so do you."

"Will you sign off on those invoices for me?"

"Sure thing. Hand 'em over." He quickly reviews them, initialing the ones I can pay.

We finish up our business, and with a quick kiss, he's out the door first. I smile, watching him and his cute butt as he goes. Sighing, I gather up the papers and hug them to my chest. Now that I have a minute, it hits me. I think I've got a boyfriend. A real one. A chill runs down my back. A real *hot* one. Who'da thunk it? Lainie Palmer landed herself a hottie.

CHAPTER TWELVE

KEETON

NEARLY FUCKING Lainie in my office was probably not my brightest idea, since I've been hard as nails ever since. Try squatting down beside a bike in that state, fellas. On second thought, don't, because I may have permanently damaged one of my favorite body parts. I think it might be worth it, though. Did I suspect Lainie was untouched? Hell, no. But, I'm not gonna lie, I'm pleased as shit. I knew that woman was for me the second she stepped foot in my office. The fact that she'll have me, and only me, makes me puff my chest out like a goddamn rooster.

I don't get back to my office from the shop until after three. I peek into Lainie's office and see the lights are out. "Shit. I forgot she was leaving early today." I'm suddenly bummed out. I rushed around in the shop to get back here sooner. I'm going to need to knock that shit off. This is my livelihood. I need to take care of that. If not for me, for her.

I shake my head. Since when did I become this fucking

pussy-whipped? I haven't even gotten my dick wet. All right, I'm feeling like an emotional yo-yo. Thankfully, my phone vibrates in my pocket. Checking the screen, I see it's Deb. "Hey, Deb."

"Hi, honey. How are you today?"

"I'm okay. Why wouldn't I be?"

"Oh, I don't know. After you called yesterday, I was curious if your new friend decided to work for you."

"Lainie? Yes. She started today."

"And?"

"And what?" Women. No matter how cool Deb acts, she's just like the rest of them when it comes to getting into my business.

In her defense, I called her first.

"And?"

"She did great."

"That's it? You're not going to expand?"

"No."

"Jesus, it's like pulling teeth. Fine. I'll just have to come see for myself, since you won't talk. Besides, you promised me a beer. Talk to you later? I'm here if you want to talk."

"Sure. Yeah. Talk to ya." I hang up the phone, shaking my head. "Women."

Since I've got nothing waiting for me in the office, I head back out to the shop. Might as well get some shit done.

CHAPTER THIRTEEN

Lainie

BY THE TIME I get to Murphy's, I'm not surprised I'm the last one to arrive. Even Agatha made it here before me. Checking my watch again, I see I'm right on time. At the table, I spy two baskets of wings, one with fries, and another with fried pickle chips. It's our standard order, but the fact it's already on the table says someone was here extra early. "I'm not late, right?"

"Nope, I just needed a drink, so I got here early," says Agatha as she raises her beer glass to her mouth.

If I didn't know better, I'd say she's been crying, but that's so not Agatha. "What's wrong?"

"She won't tell us." Keely stares at her sister with concern. "She's had an entire pitcher on her own already."

"Aggie. What's up? Spill."

Setting the glass down, I watch as her eyes well up and fresh tears pour out. "I g-got f-fired."

There's a collective gasp at the table. My workaholic sister fired? No way. "No!"

"What the hell happened?" asks Keely. She never holds back. I guess that's a good thing.

Wiping fresh tears away, Agatha takes in a deep calming breath. "They said I, er, I embezzled money."

"No fucking way." Keely again. She's the only one with a potty mouth at this table.

"That's insane," says Sadie as she moves two seats over to sit by Aggie. "Why would they think you did something so preposterous?"

We wait for her to respond. She takes a big gulp of her beer. "Money's missing. They said they followed the trail and it led right to me."

"What evidence do they have?" asks Violet.

We all know Aggie's penchant for solving puzzles. She loves reading mysteries in her spare time and prides herself on solving the crime before the book detective.

"I don't know. They wouldn't show me anything. All they said was, 'If you leave today, without another word, we won't press ch-charges.'" She starts to sob again. "Charges?" she squeaks. "Seriously? I'm not criminal."

"Honey, it was probably just some accounting error. You do work in their accounting department. I'm sure they'll find it. How much is missing?" I ask, holding her free hand.

"Over a hundred thousand."

"Dollars?!" shouts Keely. "Whoa, when you decide to turn to a life of crime, you really do it right."

"Keely!" snaps Violet.

We're all struck dumb by Violet's raised voice. We stare at her, waiting.

"Sorry," she mumbles. "Keely's joke. It wasn't helping."

No, it wasn't, but that's sort of Keely's stress mechanism.

Humor, or an attempt at it. Most of the time she gets a laugh, but not this time. This time her joke falls flat.

"What can we do?" Sadie redirects us all back to Aggie.

"Nothing," she sighs. "Well, it would help if we could change the subject." She turns to me. "What's with the email today? Why did you ask about Lewis?"

"Wait. Before we get to that," says Sadie, "don't you think it's odd they aren't pressing charges? I mean, over one hundred thousand dollars? That's not chump change."

We all stare at Sadie. No one speaks for several minutes, and it's Aggie who breaks the silence. Sniffling, she says, "I thought of that. Right now, I need to process everything before I try to wrap my head around it."

Standing up, I walk over and wrap my arm over her shoulders, giving her a squeeze. "That's a good plan, sis. We're here for you."

"I know." She wipes her nose with a napkin. "Now, can we get back to the reason you called the meeting?"

"Yeah. Tell us what Lewis-the-dick did now," grumbles Keely.

Hearing her say that makes me a little sad. Keely and Lewis used to be close. I'm pretty sure he liked her better than me, but I won't get into that. Her heart was broken the night she ran into him at *AltLyph*, a club in Flagstaff that caters to the LGBTQ community. She was there with her bestie, Michael, celebrating his birthday. When she spotted Lewis making out with one of his *friends* in a plush VIP booth, I think part of her heart broke—for me and for herself. Poor Keels.

I should have told her. I should have told the rest of them, but there was never a right time to say, "Oh, hey, by the way, my husband is gay. Don't tell anyone." So, when she saw him, she was shocked and hurt, and part of that is my fault. A small part.

"Fine. Changing the subject. Let me tell you what

happened this morning and then you can tell me your response to my email." I tell them about Lewis's enraged phone call to the shop and Keeton's theory about the phone app. I also hold up my old phone. "I charged this up for a while before I came out tonight, and look." I swipe my finger over the home page a few times until I get to the second-to-last screen. Amongst the apps I rarely use sits the same app Keeton discovered on my current phone. "See? It was on my old phone too."

Agatha clicks away on her phone. "Whoa. That's some app. I'd call it more of a surveillance tool than anything else."

"I know. It's creepy as heck."

Reading over Agatha's shoulder, Violet adds, "Even though they market it to parents, it seems over-the-top intrusive."

What's gotten into her tonight? She's more talkative than I've ever seen her in a group. "I agree." Turning back to the girls, I ask, "Can you think of anything?"

Sadie speaks first. "It always seemed strange how often he'd pop into the bakery when you were there."

"Right." I forgot about that.

"Remember you tried to plan his thirtieth surprise birthday party? He knew about that."

"And I thought I was so clandestine."

"You were," Keely pipes up. "And also too nice. Why would you throw him a surprise party? The guy's a douche."

"Because I was his wife."

Keely snorts in disgust. "Whatever."

Ignoring her, I look at Violet. "Can you think of anything?"

"Not specifically. I'm just thinking about all the emails and text messages we've sent to each other over the years. Personal stuff. He must have read those."

There's nothing Violet said in emails and text messages that needs to concern her; I just think it's the fact that her thoughts and feelings could have been read by someone other than me that bothers her.

"I'm sure if he was doing this, he didn't read everything, sweetie." But who knows?

Agatha speaks up next. "He probably knows about your degree."

"Oh," I gasp. I did my darndest to keep that a secret. I figured he'd blow a gasket if he knew I was working on a college degree. "And my investments." I pretty much tell my sisters everything, and not always to their faces. We text and email each other a lot. "Crap. I bet he knows everything."

"Can he get access to your money?"

"No. His name's not on any of that. He can't touch that."

"Don't be so sure," Aggie grumbles. "He's got money and friends in high places; anything is possible."

I'm not worried. My broker is well thought of and not from our hometown of Page, Arizona, so he'd have no reason to trust an inquiry from Lewis about my investments. I checked him out thoroughly before I hired him. But it doesn't hurt to check. I'll do that first thing in the morning. "I'll double-check. Just to be sure."

"Hey, ladies," says someone with a deep voice. We all turn to see a guy standing next to Violet. He's very attractive. Not as hot as Keeton, but who is? The cute guy turns to Violet. "Nice to see you again. It's been a while."

We all stare at her. Waiting. Does she know this guy? Sitting stock-still, Violet's face turns practically cherry red. Speaking softly, she says, "Kyle."

Kyle? Who the heck is Kyle? My sister's been holding back on me. Pfft, what'd I expect? She keeps her secrets like Gringotts vault holds Harry Potter's gold.

We all watch in stunned silence as this Kyle character leans in an inch closer to Violet. Matching her quiet tone, he says, "You look good, Vi."

"Can you all excuse me?" Standing abruptly, Violet pushes away from the table and makes a beeline for the bathroom.

We all watch her go until Kyle speaks. "If you'll excuse me, ladies. It was nice meeting you all." We watch as he follows the same path that Violet just took.

"What the fuck just happened?" Surprisingly, that was Sadie and not Keely. I guess the colorful vocabulary is catching.

"No clue," says Keely in a breathy voice. "But go, Violet, go. That guy was smokin' hot."

"He was, but Violet's reaction was strange. Don't you think?" I ask the girls.

Sadie nods, "I agree. She practically sprinted to the back of the bar."

Aggie nods as she finishes off yet another glass of beer. "And he sprinted off after her." Aggie's eyebrows move up and down. "Maybe Vi's finally gonna get some."

I stare at Agatha, because that's not something she'd normally say. It must be the beer. "A hangover isn't going to help you," I say, stating the obvious.

"Shush up, Lainie. I just need to forget for a while. Tomorrow will come soon enough. That's when I'll have to figure out how to get a job when the one I've had for the last eight years is no longer a viable reference." She pours a fresh glass from the pitcher. "No one is going to hire me. I'll have to sell my pretty little house and move in with Dad." A big, wet tear slides down her cheek.

"No. I'm sure if we put our heads together, we'll figure this out."

"No, you've got your own mystery to solve. I'll be fine." She looks at me and smiles. "I promise. The wounds are just fresh today. Tomorrow will be a better day."

Violet returns from the bathroom sans the cute guy.

"Where's Kyle?" Keely teases.

"Gone." Violet reaches out and grabs Keely's beer, drinking the entire glass in seconds.

I stare at Violet. It's then I see how hard she's working to get her breathing under control. Her face is red too. "Vi? You okay?"

"Fine." She puts down Keely's glass and picks up her own, sipping the clear liquid. Water? She hasn't been drinking much at all lately. I'd like to ask her more, but I can tell she's done talking about Kyle and whatever just happened.

"How do you know Kyle?"

"From college," she says quickly.

After graduating high school, Violet went to the University Southeast Arizona, but she quit in the middle of the year. None of us really knows why, only that she didn't like it there and Tucson was too far away from all of us. I guess that's a good enough reason. She's since returned to school attending a college close to Page.

After the food is gone and the beer has been drunk, we all hug and kiss cheeks with the promise that we'll talk soon. They all agree to email me until we know what's going on with my phone. I promise to only read them on my computer at GCM. It seems the safest course of action right now. Not only that, I don't want Lewis to get wind of Agatha's problems. He knows everyone in this town, and he's got a big mouth.

Well, dang, so much happened I didn't tell them about my date. Next time.

CHAPTER FOURTEEN

Lainie

I WAKE up bright and early with a smile on my face. Why is that, you ask? It could be due to the fact that I get to go to work to see my sexy new boyfriend. Or, how 'bout the fact that I'm no longer Lainie Palmer-Bottoms. Nope. As of four thirty yesterday afternoon, I'm plain old Lainie Palmer—at least on my driver's license. I'll have to update my voter registration card and request a new passport and social security card as soon as all the paperwork is filed with the state.

Luckily, it was pretty easy to get it done. All I needed was to get the judge to sign off on it, since I didn't request it at the time of the divorce. Thankfully, it was all pretty painless. That is, until I "ran into" Lewis at the courthouse. Now I suspect it's not actually a coincidence, I was even more guarded in my reaction to him. No doubt he knew the real reason I was at the courthouse; I'd searched changing my name on my phone and actually downloaded the forms from the state licensing site from email. How he knew I had a hearing with the judge today, of all days, remains to be seen.

When I saw him, I did my best to hide behind a big pillar in the hallway of the courthouse. Alas, it didn't work. He'd seen me.

"Well, Elaine, I thought I saw your fancy new car outside. Funny running into you here, of all places? What happened? Did you get a speeding ticket in your very *expensive* little sports car?"

First, my name isn't Elaine. It's Lainie. Lainie Caroline Palmer. It's on my birth certificate. He knows that, but he continues to call me Elaine. I think he's trying to frustrate me. It's working.

"Lewis." I attempted to walk past him. I wasn't in the mood for small talk. When he grasped my wrist, I startled. "Lewis. Get your hands off me."

Releasing me, he chuckled. "That's not what you said when we were married." It's creepy.

I had no idea what he was talking about, but suspected he wasn't alone. I scanned the lobby and saw one of his coworkers. I guess that answered my question. They still thought he was straight. I thought that maybe the reason he wanted out of the marriage was so he could finally be happy with someone else, but I guess not.

With a faux, sticky-sweet voice, he coos, "Sweetheart, I just want to make sure you're okay. Are you in trouble? Do you need my help? Money?"

"No, I'm fine. Thanks." I step away. "Goodbye, Lew." He hates when I call him Lew. See? I can play the game too.

When I get home, the first thing I do was delete that app from my phone. The second thing I do is send Keeton a text. *When did I become so bold?* It could be the time he had my panties off in his office that gave me the courage. Yeah, that's probably it. Anyway, I wanted to tell him about seeing Lewis.

Me: *Two things. 1. I deleted the app from my phone. 2. I did that after "running into" Lewis at the courthouse.*
Keeton*: Courthouse? Why were you there? You okay?*

Now, see? I didn't mind at all that *he* asked me. Lewis, not so much.

Me: *I was getting my name changed back to just Palmer. And before you pat yourself on the back, I had the appointment with the judge set up before we met.*

Two days before we met, but who's counting?

Keeton: *Me? I'd never take credit for such a thing. ;) So, how do you feel, Lainie Palmer?*
Me: *Great. I'm proud to be plain old Palmer now.*
Keeton*: There's not one damn thing that's plain about you, dollface.*

Ooh, dollface. That's a new one.

Me: *Thank you. You're very sweet.*
Keeton: *No one's ever accused me of being sweet.*
Me*: It's good. I like sweet things.*
Keeton*: Well then, consider me dipped in chocolate, just for you.*
Me*: LOL. I do love chocolate. Too much. But, you could tell that right? LOL*

When I don't get a response from him, I'm not sure what to

do. So, I just sit and stare at the stupid phone, waiting. And waiting. When it ring, it startles the phone right out of my hand.

I quickly picked it up, pressing the green button. "Hello?"

"You didn't just disparage yourself, right?"

Why would Keeton sound angry about that? He'd seen me, right? I made a combination laugh-snort sound. "Keeton. I'm a full-figured woman. You know this. *I* certainly know this."

"You're curvy and gorgeous."

"Well, thank you, that's nice of you to say, but—"

"No buts, babe. You're beautiful, and that body of yours is fucking amazing."

Amazing? That's just a tad overboard, don't you think? I can't help wondering what this guy is drinking. Wacky juice? Instead of prolonging the painful, albeit kind, conversation, I change the subject. "So, are we still on for tomorrow night?"

BY THE TIME I get to the shop the next morning, the back door is unlocked, all the lights are on, and music is playing loudly somewhere inside. The door to the showroom is closed, so the sound's muffled. Eric must be here. I step into the showroom and peek into the shop through the large window that separates both spaces. I see two guys walking around, but no Eric.

"Looking for me, sweetheart?"

I scream so loud, my head vibrates. I take a moment to catch my breath, and when I turn around, Eric is laughing so hard he's bent at the waist. "Not funny, Eric. Geesh, you scared the stuffing out of me."

With his hand on my upper back, he says, "Sorry, Lainie. I really didn't mean to startle you."

Shaking my head, I smile. "It's okay. Just don't sneak up on a girl. It's bad for our health."

"What's bad for your health?" Keeton's deep rumble comes up from behind us. "And hands off, Eric."

He quickly takes his hand off my back, raising them both like he's been caught in the cookie jar. "Just helping a damsel in distress, brother. That's all." Eric chuckles.

"That's my job," Keeton says, stomping to my side.

"Okay, well, that's enough testosterone for me first thing in the morning. I'm going to get to work." I go around both men and walk quickly into my, I mean, Molly's office.

I work the entire morning with the telephone as my only interruption. The number of calls from people angry about their bills is basically down to none. I paid all of the outstanding accounts yesterday. Today, I'm working through requests for new parts and equipment. The writing on the forms is hard to read, thanks to oil smudges and what looks like coffee stains. At least I hope it's only coffee stains. Not only that, the writing is rushed and sloppy. Couple that with my lack of knowledge of motorcycle parts and it's got the makings of a perfect storm of goof-ups.

Grabbing the stack of papers, I peek in Keeton's office, but he's not there. I think I heard him walk down the hallway earlier. I make my way out of the showroom, through the door to the shop. Scanning the large space, I see guys working. I haven't met them all yet, but a few of them have popped in to leave me purchase requests. They've all been very nice so far.

I look left and see a large archway that leads to another space. I walk through the arch into another shop altogether. This one is just as spacious as the first, but there are only two garage doors on this side. Another difference is this side seems to be where the custom bike work is done. There are parts strewn about on the floor and hanging on the walls. I look further right and see Keeton. A shirtless Keeton, squatting down next to a bike that could best be described as skeletal. From the front tire to the back tire, it's curved and shaped like a spine. Even the way all the parts of the bike were designed take on that bone-like quality. There are lines and ridges throughout the machine. It's beautiful and reminiscent of the drawing I saw in the showroom. So is the half-naked man now walking toward me.

"Hey, babe. Need something?"

I blush, and I'm not sure why. Maybe because I feel like I just trespassed on something really personal for Keeton. "These orders. Um, I can't read some of them." I pause for a second as he gets close enough to smell. Oil and him. Yummy. "That motorcycle is beautiful."

"You like it?" he says with a beaming smile.

"It's like the drawing in the showroom."

"It is. Come here." He holds his hand out for me. I place mine in his, and it feels like it belongs there. "Let me show you what I've done with this one."

"It looks like the skeleton of a ferocious animal." It's the best way to describe it. "Like it could pounce."

He stops in his tracks, turning to me. Stepping close, he smiles again. "That's exactly what I was thinking about when I designed it. No one else has gotten that yet." His lips touch mine softly once, then once more with some nibbling of my bottom lip and a swipe of his tongue for good measure. He turns toward the bike again, pulling me along with him. Gently squeezing my hand, he says, "I'm proud of this one, Lainie."

"You should be. It's amazing." It really is. I'm not just saying that.

"I tried something new with it. Wanna know what it is?"

"Sure." Not that I'll get it.

"It's a secret."

"Okay." Who am I going to tell? Violet? She knows less about cars and motorcycles than I do, and I know nothing.

"See how the front wheel is larger than the back?"

"I do. It's what makes it look pouncey, like I said."

He chuckles. "Pouncey." Kissing the hand he hasn't stopped holding, he continues. "Yeah, well, some of the custom bikes are doing that now, but I changed up the ratios so now the front wheel is 2.5 percent larger."

"Why? Besides looking cool, does it do something else?"

"Good question. The answer is yes. You get better handling with the larger tire and more torque thanks to the smaller one in the back."

"Torque? What's that?"

"Torque, hm, let me see if I can explain that in a way you'll get. It's related to acceleration. The more torque, the more quickly your bike accelerates."

I nod. "I get it. Thanks for dumbing it down for me." I laugh.

"I didn't dumb it down. You're not dumb, I just—"

I place my palm on his chest and tap gently. "Keeton, I said I appreciated it. And I do." I lean in and kiss his lips. I can't believe I just did that. I made a move—Lainie Palmer made a move. And if the way Keeton just smiled is any indication, he liked it too. "Now help me understand what the heck these PO's say. I can't read anyone's writing."

"Yeah, Molly's been at it long enough to be able to identify their scribbles. Here, hand them over, let's see what you've got."

One by one, Keeton clarifies the information on each form. A couple were so bad he had to yell at the guy who put the order in to translate. In all, I spent about a half an hour with him in his shop. I loved it.

"Well, I'm going to go place these orders. See you later?"

"I've got a client meeting over lunch. Do you want me to bring you something?"

Gosh, he's so sweet. Lewis never offered that. Heck, he didn't want me to eat.

"Nope. I still have my salad from yesterday in the fridge." I put it in there after lunch yesterday.

"You sure about that?"

"Why?"

He nods sideways toward the guys in the other shop. "They'll eat anything. Even salad."

"Oh, I'll check. It's no biggie." I'm sure I've got a granola bar from this decade at the bottom of my purse.

"Double-check. If they got to it, let me know. I'll kick their asses and bring you back something."

"It's fine."

He wraps his arms around me. "Honey. I won't have you going hungry because one of my guys ate your rabbit food. Okay?"

"Sure. Okay. I'll let you know if it's gone." No, I won't.

"Shit," he mumbles. "Why don't I believe you?" He stomps out of his shop and through the other one, shouting, "If one of you little pricks ate Lainie's salad, I'm going to kick your ass."

I'm walking behind him as fast as I can on my heels. It's not easy. "Keeton, stop. I'll check. I promise I'll tell you. It's not a big deal."

Ignoring my plea, he opens the showroom door, holding it open for me to pass through, then he passes me on the way to the fridge. Yanking the door open, he bends at the waist, searching. Grabbing my plastic container—it's pink, so I guess he figured it was mine—he holds it up in front of me. "This is it?"

"Yes."

He pops the lid open to see lettuce and two cherry tomatoes. That's all there is. I didn't have time to go to the store for more veggies. "This is it?"

"See, no one ate my lunch," I say. Just as I'm reaching for it, but he pulls it back.

"This is *it*?"

"Yes." I laugh out of frustration. "Now, give me my lunch and go to your meeting."

"Lainie, there's not enough food in here to feed a hamster."

I roll my eyes and then put my fists on either hip. I feel like stomping my foot, but I refrain. He's making me a little angry now. "Keeton Gustafson, Give. Me. My. Salad."

Blinking at me, he quickly hands it over, "Lainie, I'm sorry. I—"

"Don't worry about it," I mumble, stepping around him.

"I am worried about it. I didn't mean to make you angry."

Turning to face him, I say, "Look. My ex-husband was always in my face about what I ate. I'd just like to be able to eat my food without your opinion on the matter, okay?"

"Sure. Okay. I'm sorry, babe."

Wow, he's singing a different tune now. Not so bossy now that I've said my piece. Dang, it's refreshing. "Good. Now go to your meeting and let me get back to work."

"Right. Sure. See you this afternoon."

I walk back to my office clutching my Tupperware container with a death grip. I surprised myself with all of that back there. I never once told Lewis how I felt about his food policing. He'd never listen, anyway. I became much more passive-aggressive with him. I like that I can say what's on my mind with Keeton Gustafson. I like it a lot.

CHAPTER FIFTEEN

KEETON

I THINK I hit a nerve with Lainie. One I don't plan on hitting again. The thing is, how am I going to make sure she's gotten enough to eat without her throwing her hands in the air and walking out forever? This is an area I'm not familiar with; normally I don't give two shits if I piss off a woman, let alone worry about whether she's getting the nutrients she needs, but that's not the case here. What I do know is her fucking ex really did a number on her. The fact that the asshole has been keeping tabs on her for years is a good indicator that the guy has control issues. I knew just from the few sentences out of his mouth yesterday that he was jealous. But, just what will he do with that jealousy? I need to know more about him. I don't want to ask her about him tonight, on our first official date. That'll ruin it for her, and I won't have that.

I'm in Flagstaff today to meet with my attorney and friend, Mitch McCallister. He and I've ridden together for years, having met at a custom bike show. He asked me here to talk about a commission. He wants a bike dedicated to the McCallister clan, including their tartan and clan emblem. I've got some ideas rolling around in my head, but he promised me I could borrow some book about his family for research. I love this part of creating—delving into the history of something, or in the case of the skeleton bike (Lainie was right about that), I learned all about the bones and muscles of a large cat. Hopefully I can pick the book up today so my trip isn't a waste of time.

After a brief meeting with Mitch, I walk out with a huge leather tome that looks ancient, dedicated to the McCallister family history, half of which I can't read because it's in a Celtic language or Gaelic or something like that. Luckily, somewhere along the line, someone started translating it. So far, it looks sort of fascinating. There are drawings of battles, houses, and land, and lots of stories about the family. It's cool as hell.

Next, I head to a funky little bike shop that customizes helmets. I'm going to buy one for my girl. Can't have her on the back of my bike without a helmet—and not just any old helmet. I know exactly what I want. I saw it there a couple months ago. It's pink, but not bubblegum pink. It's sort of like a gradient of pink to gray and black. The style of the helmet looks like a vintage half-helmet, but has a sun shield that comes down to protect her entire face. On the back is a hand-painted rose. I'd love to have them add Lainie's name to the back, but I'll wait on that. I don't want to freak her out.

While I'm there, I pick her up some pink leather gloves and I contemplate a sweet leather jacket for her. I don't know her size and I learned a long time ago not to buy women clothes in the wrong size. If it's too big, they assume I think they're fat, and if it's too small, *they* think they're fat. It's a lose-lose situation. I'll just bring Lainie down here to pick something out next week. Maybe she'd enjoy getting away for an afternoon.

BY THE TIME I roll into the parking lot, it's after three. Grabbing the bouquet of pink roses I picked up for Lainie, I jog into the shop. At first, I'm not sure what to think of the scene I spy through the window into the showroom.

Eric strides up to me. "They've been in there almost an hour, just gabbing. Like women do."

I watch them for a second. "Like you know anything about women," I scoff.

"Well, when there's a baby in the room, I know to get the hell out." He chuckles.

I laugh and watch the three women. Debbie's cooing at the baby. I can't hear her, but she's making goo goo ga ga lips at Maddy. Next to her is Lainie. She's holding the baby, smiling and laughing as she snuggles with our beautiful new addition. Seeing her like that, with a child, stops my breath.

"She's a natural, huh, man?" Eric nudges my arm. "You two would make some cute little rug rats."

I turn and stare at my baby brother.

"You know, if you were thinking along those lines."

I am thinking along those lines. Now that I've seen her holding my niece, it's going to be *all* I think about.

Lainie's laughing as she holds Madalyn. Debbie is talking to her animatedly. And Molly? She's got a smile on her face too, but I know that look. She's a million miles away. "How's Molly?" I ask Eric. The two of them are close—in age and in life.

"She's puttin' on a brave face, man. If it weren't for Maddy, I'd be concerned about what she'd do."

My head jerks back to my brother. "You serious?"

"Well, wouldn't you be tempted if you lost the love of your life?"

I look at Lainie again. She's got Madalyn snuggled up to her chest and neck. Her eyes are closed. I can tell she's sniffing that kid. Babies do smell pretty damn good, most of the time. She smiles at my sister and hands Maddy back. Debbie spots me first, then Molly, then Lainie. All three women smile our way.

"Now that there is a group of fine-lookin' women." I didn't hear him come up, but that comment is coming from Billy.

"They sure are, Billy Bob Thornton." Not his name, but that's what we call him because he hates it.

"I'd take any of them fine pieces of—"

I growl loudly enough for him to hear.

"Calm down, Keet. I was going to say fine pieces of lovely lady-ness."

Eric cracks up while punching Billy in the arm. Hard. "That's not a word, you dumb ass."

Ignoring the morons, I walk into the showroom.

"Hey, Keeton, honey." Deb walks up, wraps her arms around my neck, and kisses my cheek. It's a guise, because she whispers in my ear, "I love her. She's perfect."

I nod and smile at Lainie and Molly. Patting Deb's back, I walk over to my sister and take hold of Madalyn, kissing Molly's cheek. I do the same to Maddy, lingering a little longer on her chubby cheek. I do what Lainie just did and sniff her sweet skin and hair.

"She smells good, doesn't she?" Lainie says as she places her hand on the top of Maddy's head. "There's nothing like a baby to put things into perspective, huh?"

"Damn straight." I look into Lainie's eyes, "I can see clear as day when I've got Maddy in my arms."

"So, Keeton, Lainie tells me she's filling in for me."

"Yep."

"And that you've just thrown her to the wolves. No training, Keet?"

"I trained her."

"It took me months to get that job down." Her brows furrow, then she sighs. "I guess Maddy and I can come in tomorrow for a couple of hours to walk you through some end-of-month stuff."

"Really? That'd be great. Bring your lunch so we can chat some more while we eat."

"Better yet, we can go out to lunch on Keet's dime." Molly smiles a real smile.

Hell yes, I'll buy her lunch if it makes her smile. I'm watching the three women and one baby girl in my life, and I smile too. This feels good. It feels right.

Deb leaves first. "Lainie, it was so nice to meet you. I hope to meet your sisters sometime too. They sound really cool."

"They are. Let me know when you'll be in town next, and I'll plan something."

"Awesome." Deb gives Lainie a hug, kisses Maddy on the forehead, and gives my sister an even bigger hug. "I'm here for you, sis," she says softly to Molls.

"I know," Molly whispers in reply.

"Walk me out, Keet."

"Sure thing." I follow Debbie out to the parking lot to her vintage 1965 Ford Mustang convertible, cherry red. It was her dream car for years. I'm glad to see she finally got it.

"Nice ride."

"I know, right?" She smirks. "She's a beast. It's got a two-eighty-nine with a four-barrel."

"Jesus, I bet she hauls ass."

"That she can." She laughs. "So, I'm going to say one thing."

I knew this was why she wanted to walk me out. "Okay."

"Marry that girl. Invite me to the wedding. Have lots of babies with her. Make me a godmother. But you'd better move quick. She's a keeper."

"Shit, you're freaking me out."

"Good." She kisses my cheek, slides into her ride, flicks it to life, and tears out of my parking lot.

"Now there goes a damn good woman." Maybe she'll find the one for her someday. Oh, shit. When did I turn into a pussy? *About three days ago, if I'm counting.*

Back in the shop, Molly's the only one in the lounge area. "Hey, how're you doing? Really?"

"Shitty." She's putting Maddy in her baby carrier. "But I just joined a group for spouses of soldiers who died in service. It's nice to talk to people who've been through the same thing."

"That's good. If you ever need me to watch Maddy while you take care of yourself, I'm there."

She sniffles. "I know. And I love you and Eric for everything you've done. I wouldn't have made it without you."

"You always have us." I pick up the baby carrier and follow her out.

At her car, she says, "Tell Lainie I'll see her tomorrow."

"I will."

Snapping Maddy into her seat, she adds, "I like her, Keeton. She's kind, gentle, and beautiful."

"Deb told you?"

"Of course. Just trust me, big brother. Grab on to her and don't let go." Molly's crying now. "You think you have all the time in the world, but you don't." I wrap my arms around her. "I'm okay, Keet. Just get back in there and do what I say."

"Yes, ma'am."

I watch her pull out of the lot and feel a warm hand on my arm. "Your ex-wife is amazing and cool. I can see why you get along so well with her."

"Yeah, she's okay." I turn to face her. Bringing my arms around her, I pull her to me. Sighing, I realize it's been hours since I've even touched her.

"Your sister is so nice and pretty. And that baby, Keeton. So beautiful."

"She is."

"I can see Madalyn's got Molly's mouth, but her eyes.... Do they look like her daddy's?"

I'm quiet for a minute. I'm not sure if she knows. "She looks a lot like Adam."

"Where is he?" She looks toward the shop. "Does he work here?"

Nope, they didn't tell her. "Adam... Adam is dead."

"Oh, no!" she says, shocked. "How?"

"He was an Army Ranger. He was killed in Afghanistan a week before he was done."

"Oh, no." Lainie's voice has gotten so soft. Her chin and bottom lip are quivering. "Did he get to m-meet her?"

"No, baby." I swipe a tear that just slid down her cheek.

"I-I think that's just about the saddest thing I've ever h-heard." She's full-on crying now. "Poor Molly," slips out between sobs. "And Maddy."

I hold her tight against me, running my palm up and down her back, attempting to soothe her. "Shh, it's okay. Molly's strong. She's got all of us to support her to love her and Maddy."

"I know," she cries, "but it's not the s-same."

"Shh, honey. I know. Adam was my best friend. We all miss him. It's a loss we feel every day."

"Your best f-friend?" she wails. "Oh, my gosh, Keeton. I'm so sorry. It makes my troubles seem so insignificant. My heart breaks for all of you."

I know she means it. Her heart is all in with the people she cares about—even people she just met. "How'd I get so lucky to meet you?"

She blinks up at me. Tears are clinging to her long lashes, mascara staining her cheeks. "Really?"

"Really. Now, come on. Let's close up shop. We've got a date tonight."

"Oh." She sounds disappointed. "I'm not sure I'm up for a date now."

Oh, well damn. "Another night?" I was looking forward to it.

"Why don't you come over to my place. I'll cook dinner. I'm sure my sister can find someplace to go."

She lives with her sister? I guess I knew that, since she's driving her car—or she was. "Let's go to my place. I'll cook dinner for *you*. I've got some steaks in the fridge. We'll watch a movie and be cozy."

No fucking way did I just say *cozy*.

"That sounds nice. I want to go home and change first."

"I'll pick you up at seven like we planned and give you a ride on my bike back to my house."

"Yes!" she says excitedly. "That's perfect."

Walking hand-in-hand back through the shop, I spot the flowers I bought her. I must have set them down. "Oh, I bought you these."

"Pink roses?"

"When I think of a color for you, it's pink."

"I love pink." She smells the bouquet. "Thank you. No one has ever bought me flowers before."

Jesus, what did that piece of shit husband ever do for her? I know he wasn't sleeping with her, but he could have at least been nice to her. I'm not getting into that now. No way. It's date night and I'm taking my girl home with me. Maybe I can even talk her into staying. Forever.

CHAPTER SIXTEEN

Lainie

I'M SO NERVOUS. I've nibbled off the rest of the pink polish on my thumb waiting for Keeton. I'm listening for the rumbling of his motorcycle while I surreptitiously peek out the window through Keely's blinds.

"Will you sit down, girl? You're making *me* nervous," says Keely as she flips television channels.

"I can't help it. It's like my first *real* date." I'm not counting the one with Tod Mendenhall now. This is the first real one.

"Do you know how weird that sounds coming from a divorcée?"

Divorcée? Definitely a 1950s word, and one that makes breaking up with your gay husband sound glamorous. It's not. Trust me. "I know how strange it sounds. My entire life, up to this point, has been strange."

Keely laughs. "It's still strange." Sipping her glass of three-buck chuck from Trader Joe's, she adds, "My oldest and prissiest sister is going on a date with a biker dude. If that isn't fucked-up, I don't know what is."

It's my turn to laugh. "Wait 'til you meet him. You'll get it."

"I won't get to meet him. Not tonight, anyway. You think he's going to walk up here to pick you up? He's a biker, hon. He'll honk, then yell 'Lainie!' at the top of his lungs until you run down there."

We live in a three-story building in the older part of town. It was built in the 1960s or 70s, when they thought it'd be cool to have a lot of open spaces for people to "commune." When you open our front door, there's a walkway that everyone takes to the stairs. Like an old motel. From our side of the building, I can see the parking lot perfectly. She may be right, but I don't think so. "No, he won't. You'll see."

"If that biker dude walks up three flights of stairs to escort you down for your date, you should probably marry him. Either that or I'll eat my socks."

"Ha ha." The sock part is funny, but the marriage part? Not so funny. I'm already so into him, I could see myself jumping into marriage even though I know it's probably a bad idea. Heck, I'm planning on jumping into bed with him on the first date. How's that for an indication of how much this guy affects me.

When I hear the rumble of a motor, I gasp. "He's here."

"In order for this little experiment to work, you can't let him see you at the window. So, step back and let's see what he does."

The motor shuts off, and I turn to Keely with a knowing smirk. When we don't hear anything for several minutes, Keely rolls off the couch and stands next to me. Booted footsteps sound on our level and get louder the closer they get to our door. I squeeze Keely's hand like my life depends on it. "I'm so nervous," I whisper.

"You work with him," she whispers back. "You see him every day."

"I know." I do know, but this feels different. Very different.

When the knock sounds on the door, we both jump, startled. "You get it," I whisper to Keely. "I'll go back into the hallway for a minute."

Keely giggles softly. "Okay. This is so fun." She straightens her beloved Elvis Costello concert tee and swipes a hand over her long hair.

I quickly walk back far enough down the hall so he can't see me, but stay close enough to hear everything.

"Coming," she says loudly, but not too loudly since she's at the door already.

I hear the door open, and I swear Keely gasps. "You must be Keeton. I'm Keely."

In a low, sexy, rumbly voice, Keeton speaks. "Nice to meet you. You the owner of the blue Honda?"

"Oh, yeah. What's up with that?"

I hear Keeton make a noise like a grumble. "Piece of shit, girl. How 'bout we talk about this later. Where's Lainie?"

"Right here," I singsong as I walk into the main room. I spot him, and I want to drool. He's so dang hot in his dark jeans, deep blue dress shirt, and black leather jacket that looks worn and soft. *Yummy.* I look at his clean-shaven face and smile. "Hi."

"Hi," he says, smiling at me like he likes the look of me. "You look beautiful, babe."

He must be crazy. All I did after work was brush my teeth and hair, freshen up my makeup, and change into jeans and a flowy pink top with tiny multicolored flowers embroidered all over it. I like it because it makes my chest look nice with a deep V-neck, while also being long enough and flowy enough to hide my stomach and hips. "Are these boots okay?" I chose to wear some high-heeled booties because I read that it's best to wear boots on a motorcycle. Besides, these are adorable.

"Fuck yeah. You look sexy as hell."

"Holy shit," Keely mumbles. Walking past me, she whispers, "Marry him, or I will."

I laugh at her but keep looking at my date. "You look nice too."

He holds out his hand, and I see he's holding daisies. I think daisies are quite possibly the most romantic flower *ever*. Those are the "he loves me, he loves me not" flowers. "Oh, Keeton. I love daisies. Thank you." I take them from him, letting my fingers brush against his. I don't know if I'll ever get used to the chills I get whenever we touch.

Keely's back, taking the flowers from me. "I'll put them in some water for you, sis."

"I didn't want to give you roses again." He smiles sweetly.

"Again? You already gave her roses?" Keely says from the kitchen sink. "Geez, you've known each other three days."

He shrugs. "She deserves flowers."

Keely steps up to him holding a vase full of daisies. She works fast. Patting him on his leather-clad shoulder, she says, "That she does, my good man. That she does."

"Shall we?" Keeton's hand is reaching toward me. I place mine in it and move with him toward the front door.

I snatch my jean jacket off the chair as we walk out. Keeton stops to help me put it on. "We'll need to get you a leather jacket."

"Why?"

"It looks cool." He chuckles. "I saw one for you today but didn't buy it because I learned a long time ago, from my sister, that you ladies need to pick things out yourselves."

"Right." Thank goodness he didn't buy me a jacket. How humiliating would it have been if it was too small? Super humiliating. It's happened repeatedly to me at Christmastime. Lewis would buy me some kind of dress or sweater that was two sizes too small. Then he'd say, "It's probably too small, but that's just a good goal for you. Right?"

I always nodded because we were usually in front of either his family or mine. See? Humiliating. Side note: none of those things ever fit, goal or no goal. I returned most of them without Lewis knowing and bought things I liked. So, Keeton's right. Smart man.

Before shutting the door all the way, Keely gets the last word. "Don't do anything I wouldn't do." She cackles.

"She's funny," Keeton says, smirking.

"Oh, yeah, she's hysterical." I laugh. "She's the baby and the most outspoken and most determined one of the bunch. She's also the smallest."

"You're the prettiest," he says, kissing my hand.

"How do you know? You've only met Keely."

He shrugs. "I just do. Don't question me, woman."

I roll my eyes and follow him down the steps to his bike. It's not the one from earlier. This one is bigger, a lot bigger, and a matte black color. "How many motorcycles do you own?"

He looks up, thinking. "Ten?"

"Ten? Ten motorcycles?"

"Well, sure. It's my job. How would it look if I showed up places on the same bike all the time? This one is called a touring bike. It's longer, wider, and the seats are more comfortable for long rides."

I giggle. "You sound like a woman with her shoes."

He arches his brow and pulls me to him. "I'm no woman, honey."

Feeling his body against mine, with all of his hardness, I say, "Oh, I know."

"Good." Releasing me, he opens a boxlike compartment at end of the motorcycle. "This is for you."

It's a helmet. An adorable helmet. "Is this the helmet all your ladies wear when they're on the back of your bike?"

"First of all, I bought that helmet today, just for you. Second, the last woman who rode on the back of my bike was Molly. The one before that, Deb, about fifteen years ago." Stepping close to me, he places the helmet on my head. Next, he snaps the chin strap in and adjusts it so it fits correctly. In a deep, sultry voice, he finishes with the best one yet. "And third, you're the only one I want, Lainie."

"Okay," I whisper. I lean forward and kiss his lips. "Thank you for the helmet. It's super cute."

"You're super cute." He chuckles. "I knew it was perfect for you. Pink is your color."

"I do love pink." I watch as Keeton slides over, straddling his bike. I'm not sure what to do now.

"Put your hand on my shoulder, here," he says, patting his leather-clad shoulder.

I do as he instructs.

"Place your left foot on that foot peg there," he points to the tube-like thing coming out from the side of the motorcycle. "Hold on to me and swing your right leg over the back of the bike."

I'm not the most athletic person in the world, but I do as he says, and my leg goes right over. "I did it!"

"You did. Great job. Now scoot as close to my back as you can and bring your arms around my middle."

I do as he instructs, and he pats my hands in approval. "Keep them here. Hold on tight. When I lean to turn, you do too. Okay?"

"Okay," I reply nervously. Why is this so scary?

"Ready?"

"Ready."

He hits a button on his handlebars, and the motorcycle

comes to life with a roar and a rumble. The vibrations are running through my entire body. Keeton pushes the bike off the stand, and it begins to move out of my parking lot, then out onto the street. In no time, we're on the old highway and heading out of town at a fast clip. It's exhilarating. I press my body into his and make a "woo-hoo" sound. I feel him chuckling through my fingers. His belly's rumbling with me. My goodness, this feels amazing. I'm surrounded by sensations. The rumble of the bike, the vibration of the road beneath me, the feel of his hard muscles under my hands and my chest. And his smell—*my, my, my*, his smell. It's musky and sexy and all man, all Keeton.

In no time, he's slowing the bike down and we're pulling off the highway onto a gravel road. Or at least I think it's a road. He's driving slowly on a long, curvy lane surrounded by trees. When I see lights up ahead, I realize it's a driveway. Past the last grove of trees, a sprawling house comes into view. It's big. The roofline is tall, and there are four dormer windows along the top, telling me there's an upper level. I count four garages.

Keeton pauses as one of the doors opens in front of us. Pulling in, he parks the motorcycle in the same bay as a few other bikes. When he turns off the motor, it's quiet enough that I can finally speak. "This is your house, Keeton?"

"Yep. All mine."

"It's amazing," I say breathlessly. "Seriously amazing."

Keeton squeezes my hands, which are still holding tight to his stomach. "I'm glad you like it, Lainie. That's important to me." He pats my hands again. "Okay, now hop off the same way you got on. Hold on to my shoulder, place your foot on the peg, and swing your leg back over."

"Oh, geesh, Keeton." I put my hands on his shoulders and try to stand up, but I can't seem to do it. "What if I fall and pull you along with me?"

"You won't, honey. Do you trust me?"

"Yes, of course."

"Okay, then hang on. Put your hands behind you. Hold on to the seat back."

Uh-oh, I don't like the sound of that, but I watch as he swings his leg over the front of the bike, stepping off like it's the easiest thing in the world. The next thing I know, his left arm is beneath my legs and his other is around my waist and he's lifting me up. "No!" I yelp. "Your back."

"Shh."

And then I'm on my feet, standing in front of him with my hands on my hips. "Keeton Gustafson. You cannot pick me up like that. I'm too heavy."

"You're not."

"I am. I wouldn't forgive myself if you injured yourself doing that." Or speak to him or show my face at the shop ever again. Not without everyone knowing the fat girl broke Keeton. No. Thank. You. I half expect him to argue with me, but he just laughs, grabbing my hand as he does, and pulls me toward a door that presumably leads into his house. He's so frustrating.

When the door opens, I gasp. "Oh, my gosh."

"You like it?"

I'm speechless. We've walked into a kitchen that belongs on the cover of a home decorating magazine. It's all metal and natural stone, a cook's dream.

"Do you like to cook, Lainie?" Keeton says close to my ear. I'm not sure when he came up behind me.

"I love cooking."

"Good," he says, patting my bottom. "Me too. Come on. Let me show you the rest of the house. Then we can cook together."

I nod and follow him through a very large open living area with a big sectional sofa, chairs, coffee table, and a large television mounted above a sleek black fireplace. This room feels very

Keeton-esque, if there's such a thing. I look left at large windows and walk toward them. "You've got a pool?"

"Yeah." He chuckles. "I couldn't stop adding shit to the design."

"You designed this?" I say, shocked. But why would I be shocked? He's a designer, of motorcycles, sure, but I take it from this that he has many talents.

I blush at my unintentional double entendre.

"I did, but after I drew out my rough plan, I handed it over to a professional."

"It's amazing, Keeton."

"Come on, there's lots more to see."

And there is. There are three large bedrooms on the main level, along with a huge master bedroom. When we step into the room, a chill runs down my spine. This is it. This is his bedroom. I should be more nervous, since I've done nothing but picture Keeton wearing only a smile since the second I met him. Hell, I've never wanted to lick someone so much in my entire life, which is really weird because, dang it, he's not an ice-cream cone. I can't explain the thoughts I've got rolling around in my head—thoughts related to all of the things I want to do with him.

"Here's the master bathroom."

Luckily, he's redirected my thoughts to his equally impressive bathroom and his bathtub—a bathtub so big and so deep I could cry. And it's got jets! I picture myself soaking in that thing for hours, or perhaps the two of us in there together. I do my best to shake the thought of Keeton naked *and* wet and follow him upstairs to a large open loft space that he's turned into an office and workout room. At one end is a drafting table, desk and computer, filing cabinets, and a large printer. At the other end is every weight machine I've ever seen at the Y. Well, not every weight machine, but he's got at least six different pieces of equipment plus a stationary bike and treadmill. No wonder he's in such good shape. There's a large television mounted to the wall in this room as well. It's in the perfect spot. It can be seen when he's in the office and when he's working out.

Next, we head to the basement, to what he calls the game room. I'd call it the family room times ten. There's large seating area with another large sectional and a television, but there's also an area with a pool table, foosball table, a pinball machine, a poker table, juke box, and an old-time video game machine. "Is that a Pac-Man machine?"

"It is, but you can actually choose between Pac-Man, Centipede, Frogger, Donkey Kong, Space Invaders, and Dig Dug."

"Dig Dug?" I practically shout. "I loved Dig Dug."

"You want to play?"

I smile wide. "Later. Show me the rest of the place."

"There's another bedroom down here and a full bath."

Wow. This place is huge. We step through the french doors to a large patio area that wraps around the pool.

"Is that a hot tub?"

"Yep. Wanna take a dip?" He doesn't laugh, so I think he's serious.

"Maybe later." Not really. I didn't bring a swimsuit, so that's a no.

Back inside, he leads me upstairs to the kitchen. "Let's get cookin', good-lookin'," he says, pulling out a package of meat from the fridge.

"How can I help?"

"You wanna make the salad?"

"Okay."

"Come on over here. Everything is in the fridge. You choose what you want in it. I'll eat anything, so you pick."

As I grab lettuce, carrots, green peppers, tomatoes, and

celery out of his huge sub-zero refrigerator, Keeton turns on music. It's coming from speakers mounted inside the walls. "Oh, I love this song." He's turned on some 70s ballad that I remember my dad listening to a lot.

"Little River Band," he mumbles.

"My dad used to listen to them. I like this era of music."

Leaning over to me, he kisses the top of my head. "Good. I'm glad."

It's the sweetest gesture and one that fills me with so much joy I can't even explain it. For a second, I forget the fact I want to jump his delectable bones. I smile over at him as he seasons the steaks. They're huge. I'm not sure what cut of meat it is or why he thinks I could ever eat a steak that size, but I refuse to analyze it.

"You want a beer? Glass of wine?"

"Sure. Wine sounds nice."

He bends down to open the door of a wine refrigerator that he's got installed under the counter. "What's your preference? Sweet, dry?"

"Dry, white, if you've got it."

He pulls out a bottle of Chardonnay and pours me a glass, then goes back to the big fridge and gets a beer for himself. Holding up his bottle, he smiles. "Toast."

I lift my glass to touch his beer bottle.

"To first dates."

"To first dates," I repeat. Our glasses tinkle as they touch. We both sip, staring into each other's eyes.

He holds his beer out again. "To many more."

I swallow like there's a cotton ball stuck in my throat. "To many more." I touch his bottle with my glass and smile. That moment was sort of serious. I sense that he meant it. I return to making salad as he takes out a fresh head of cauliflower. He cleans it and chops it up into chunks. "What're you making with the cauliflower?"

"Mashed potatoes."

"Huh?" I chuckle. "Don't you need potatoes for that?"

Setting down his knife, he turns to me slowly with the most serious expression I've seen yet. "You've never had mashed cauliflower potatoes?"

"No? I thought you were joking."

"Oh, babe," he says, stalking toward me. "You're going to love these. All the goodness of mashed potatoes without the starch."

"You eat low carb?"

He pats his stomach. "I try, but I can't stop myself from eating bread, so I do stuff like this," he points at the white vegetable, "to balance it out."

"Makes sense."

This time he doesn't kiss my head, he leans down and kisses my lips. "I love seeing you in my kitchen, Lainie."

"Oh, yeah?" I love being in his kitchen.

"Yeah."

And that's it. He gets back to work, starting a pan of water to boil on his high-tech stove while I continue to chop veggies. We work well together in his state-of-the-art kitchen. "How do you like your steak, Lainie?"

"Medium is fine."

Arching his brow, he pauses before saying, "I don't want your steak to be just 'fine,' honey. Is that really how you like it?"

I look over at him. Lewis used to order my steak medium, never asking me how I preferred it. He liked it medium. "Well, I like it more on the rare side. Medium rare?"

"Got it."

While he fires up the grill, I'm tasked to prep some Italian bread to toast on the grill. It's a lot of food. I'm used to only eating the salad portion of this meal. When everything's ready, Keeton leads me to a small table off the kitchen. He's got a candle burning as he dims the lights slightly. Romantic.

He serves me a plate with a small portion of my larger steak, some of the cauliflower mashed potatoes, bread, and a bowl of salad. I wait for him to sit down before I dig in. When he does, his plate mirrors mine. "This looks delicious, Keeton. Thank you."

"You're welcome. Eat up. Plenty more in the kitchen."

I sip my wine as I watch him dig in. I cut the end off my steak and see that it's perfect. Raising the fork to my mouth, I look over to see Keeton staring. "What?" I say before the food has reached my mouth.

"I'm watching to see if you like it." He nods like he's urging me on.

Biting into the tender meat, I close my eyes and moan. "Mmm." It's delicious. I'm not sure what spices he used, but it's the right mixture of salty and savory. "So good."

When I open my eyes, he's still staring. "What?"

"My cock has been hard since I saw you at your place. When you made that sound just now, I nearly came in my jeans like a teenage boy."

"Oh." I blink a few times, attempting to wrap my head around that statement. My face is red. I don't even need a mirror for that one. He's said something deeply personal as well as sexual; I'm not sure what to say to that. "I'm sorry?"

He throws his head back, laughing. "Jesus, don't be sorry, honey. It's all good."

"Oh. Right. Okay."

"Try the mashed potatoes."

I pick up a fork and sweep some up. He's watching me again. Sliding the fork in my mouth, I wrap my lips around it and savor the flavor. "Mm," I say around the utensil.

I hear the clink-clank of silverware and look over to see he's dropped his fork. "Honey, I don't think I can wait. I've wanted you since the second you stepped into Molly's office."

I nod slowly. "Me too." I can't believe I just admitted that.

"I mean it, Lainie. I want you. Now." His voice is commanding but not loud.

"I want you too."

That must be all he needs to hear because he's up, rounding the table, and standing in front of me in seconds. He bends slightly, holding his hand out for me to take. "Come on, honey."

Oh, wow. This is it. It's happening.

Reaching out for me, he takes hold of my hand, urging me up out of my chair. I set my napkin on the table and follow him as he leads me in the direction of his master suite. I should balk, pull back, but I don't want to. I want him as much as he seems to want me. Maybe more.

CHAPTER SEVENTEEN

KEETON

THE WOMAN HAS BEEN DRIVING me crazy from the second I saw her at her place. I wasn't kidding about that. I've been rock-hard for well over an hour. But, goddamn, the moaning sounds she made when she tasted the cauliflower were the last straw. It's fucking time. I need to make her mine before I lose my mind.

Her hand is in mine as I gently pull her down the hallway to my bedroom. Inside, I lead her to the bed, moving her to stand with her back to me. I'm so pent-up, I'm not sure where to start, so I decide to touch first. Placing my palms on her ass, I squeeze gently. She gives me one of those moans again, and it undoes me. "Fuck," I growl. "I need you. I won't be able to take this slow the first time, Lainie."

"Okay."

Reaching around her, I slide my hands beneath her top, up to her tits. I feel lace beneath my fingers and hard nipples attempting to break free. I squeeze them and run my fingers over the hard little nubs, and she moans again. Fuck. She's killing me. "Off. Top off." God, I sound like a fucking cave man who can't say more than two words at a time. But she does it. I guess she speaks Neanderthal. My lucky day.

She grasps the bottom of her top and lifts it over her head, letting it drop to the floor. I'd love to look at her pretty light pink bra, but that'll have to wait. She unlatches it, and the bra pulls forward. I slide the straps from her shoulders and toss it off next to her shirt. My hands find their way to her breasts, and it's my turn to moan.

"Fuck, honey. Such sweet tits." I use my hands to turn her to face me. I need to see them, her. When she's in front of me, she tenses up. But I don't let that stop this. She'll loosen up as soon as she realizes I mean everything I'm saying.

I kiss her lips softly at first. Her tongue pokes out at me, and it's the invitation I need to go deeper, taking her mouth like I want to take the rest of her. The kiss becomes frantic. I pull away and bend further, swiping my tongue over a hard nipple. They're a deep pink, just like I imagined them. Suckling her into my mouth, I knead the other one, pinching and tugging on the tip. Switching sides, I do the same. It's not enough. I need more of her. Standing up to my full height, I look down at her. "Take your jeans, off, Lainie."

In a tiny voice, she replies, "W-what about you?"

"Me? You want me naked?" Fuck yes. I tear off my shirt and throw it behind me, not caring where the fuck it lands. Kicking off my boots, I unbutton my jeans and push them and my boxer briefs straight down, catching my socks along the way. I've never been as desperate to fuck someone as I am right now. I've got no suave moves in this moment. It's all about getting inside her. She's watching me, her eyes large and round. There's no time to analyze what she must be thinking. "Lainie, honey, strip. Please."

"Oh." She opens her jeans and slides the zipper down, revealing light pink lace panties.

They match her bra. Nice. The jeans come off first, and I wait, but she doesn't make the move to remove the lace. She's chewing on her bottom lip like she's thinking. Is she freaked out? I growl. This is no time to be thinking. No. It's time to be fucking.

Gently grasping her shoulders, I guide her down to the bed. "Lainie?" She looks up at me. She's been staring at my cock this whole time. "What's going on in that pretty head of yours?"

Raising her hand, she points at my cock. "Y-your penis is large. Very large."

Chuckling, I lean down and kiss her lips. "No worries. I promise to make this good for you. I'll go as slow as you need."

"No. Seriously. I've got a, an, uh, tool that's sort of big, and I can't really use it."

What the hell is she talking about? "You have a dildo?"

"I have Bob."

"Bob?" Who the fuck is Bob?

"Battery operated boyfriend."

"A dildo."

She nods. What? She can't say dildo? God, she's precious. I run my fist over my hard-on and look down at her. "I promise, baby, it'll fit. I'll get you nice and ready for me, okay?"

She nods again.

"Scoot into the middle of the bed. Lie back."

As she does, I take the opportunity to look at her. *Really* look at her. God, she's so fucking gorgeous. Her skin practically glows, it's so pale and soft-looking. I've already touched parts of her, so I know just how soft she is. Placing my hands on the bed, I lean over her legs, starting at her ankle, and begin slow kisses up from there. Moving from one leg to the other, up, up, up I go. When I get to her pretty pink lace, I linger there. Inhaling. So, so pretty. I slide my fingers into the waistband of her panties and slowly slide them down. She's lifted her hips slightly to help me. I'm half surprised she hasn't tried to stop me, so when I look up at her lidded gaze, I know she's ready for this. "We're taking this to the next level, baby. You understand?"

"Yeah." Her voice is soft and breathless—sexy as fuck. "I understand."

Pulling off the only clothing she had left, I drop them on the floor at my feet. Placing my knee on the bed, I prowl up her body, nudging her legs apart as I go. When our centers meet, I lean down and take her mouth. "How'd I get so lucky?" I ask between kisses.

"I don't know; this whole thing is pretty surreal to me."

"Well, let's make that dream a reality, shall we?" I don't wait for an answer as I kiss and nibble down the side of her neck. She turns her head to give me more room, telling me she likes this. My hands have a mind of their own, running up and down from her hips to the sides of her breasts, taking a moment to squeeze and tease her pink tips.

"Keeton," she moans.

Moving my hands down and behind her, I place them on her ass, squeezing as I move my mouth down. Repeating my moves from before, I spend extra time on each tit. "So fucking beautiful, Lainie."

I kiss her full belly, licking her belly button as I go. Pulling one hand away from her gorgeous ass, I run my finger along her slit. "So wet, honey."

"Yeah?" She's panting, and it's sexy as hell.

I slide my finger through her again, finding her clit already peeking out for me. I circle it, then run my finger over the top of it. I repeat that, starting slowly and building up steam with each pass. Lainie is writhing on the bed, her legs opening wider for me. "Don't stop, Keeton. Please," she whines. God, I could get used to this, to her.

As I work her clit, now with my thumb, I pump a finger into her.

"Oh, shit. Keeton."

She actually cussed? No stopping me now.

I add another finger to the mix—it's a tight fit—and I move in and out of her, searching for that elusive spot. When she squeaks, I know I've got it. I work it faster as I run my tongue over her hard clit. "Fuck!" she shouts as she comes hard. She's clenching around my fingers, squeezing them so hard I wonder if I'll get them back.

Kissing her mound, I look up at my woman. She's smiling at me. No, smiling isn't good enough; she's fucking beaming.

"Feel good?"

"Yes, God. Wow."

"Well, let's see if we can top that one, huh?" Her eyes double in size. "Shh, no worries. You're dripping down here, and you're relaxed. Ready?"

"Yes. I'm ready."

I reach over to my nightstand and grab a foil packet. Biting the edge, I rip it open, pulling the condom out as fast as fucking possible, and roll it down my length. I move my cock into place and slowly start to slide in. When she winces, I stop. Wait. She nods, and I move in again. We repeat this until I'm all the way inside and ready to fucking come already. So goddamn tight. When I feel her relax, I look into her eyes. "You okay, Lainie?"

"Yes. Can you move now, please?"

Without a word, I pull almost all the way out and back in slowly. I do this until I've worked up my speed. "Good?" I can hardly talk.

"Yes. Harder, please."

Damn, she's so fucking polite. "Harder?"

"Yes. Please."

I can't disappoint, so I pump into her so hard, her entire body is shifted to the other side of my big bed. I grasp her hands and pull them up above her head. "Hang on to the headboard." She grasps a wood slat with each hand, and that's when I really start to move. And Jesus, it's the best fuck of my life. My head is swimming as I pound into her like a madman. "Lainie, you feel so good." I pump in and out like this is the last time I'll get to do this. "I'm close. Are you?"

She's whimpering and nodding.

"Fuck, Lainie. I'm going to come so deep inside you. You want that, baby?" Holy hell, I wish I were bare. For the first time in my life I want to empty myself inside a woman. I want a kid with her. "Fuck."

"Yes!" she says, squeezing my cock like a champ. She likes the sound of that.

It hurts so fucking good. Three more thrusts, and I hear her scream out my name. I come so hard my brain feels like it explodes right along with my cock. "Shit," I pant, looking down at my woman. "So good." Leaning down, I kiss her. "You okay?"

"Uh-huh." She's sucking in gulps of air. "I can't believe I've missed out on that for my entire life."

"You aren't going to miss it anymore now that you've got me." *Mine.*

Releasing the slats on my headboard, Lainie brings one of her hands to my face, touches it gently, then moves the hand down over my heart. It's still beating fast and furiously. She traces my tattoos, her hand moving down further, over my abdominals. "You're so beautiful, Keeton."

I smile, but I'm too busy watching her hand to say anything. I'm still inside her, and the lower her hand moves, the more my dick twitches to life. Reaching around, she slides her hand over my ass, and that's pretty much all I need to go again.

"Oh. Wow. Again?"

Pulling out, I remove the condom and tie off the end. I pause with my hand on the nightstand drawer. Damn, it's tempting to go bare, but I'd better not. We haven't talked about any of this. Grabbing the condom closest, I wrap myself up tight. "We're just getting started, honey." Patting her hip gently, I say, "Roll over, up on your knees. Hang on to the headboard."

"Keeton. I don't know."

"Trust me. This will feel amazing."

She nods and moves into place. I run my palms over her pale, round ass. It's as soft as the rest of her. When I thrust inside her, we both moan loudly. "So deep," she mumbles.

So fucking deep.

CHAPTER EIGHTEEN

Lainie

WOW. I have no words right now. Okay, I do have words, I'm just not sure I have the energy to say them. *Wow.* That's about the only thing my brain can process right now. Making love with Keeton Gustafson is beyond words. I knew sex would feel good, but I had no idea it could feel that good. After the second time, I watched him stride confidently to the bathroom. His backside is amazing, and his muscled back flexed as he walked. But the return view was even better, and he brought a warm washcloth. He used it on me to soothe my lady parts. We used protection, but I'm not going to lie; part of me wished he hadn't worn a condom. I've always wanted a family. But having unprotected sex is irresponsible, especially for someone my age. And with a man I barely know. Heck, I don't even know if he wants children. Yep. Definitely irresponsible.

Right now, I'm snuggled up against the most gorgeous, sweetest, sexiest man I've ever seen. His big arms are wrapped around me, holding me to him, and my head is on his chest. His breathing has slowed and gotten sort of rhythmic. He's sleeping. I need to do that too. I'm tired from everything, but I'm afraid if I go to sleep, I'll wake up and this will all have been a dream. I poke my head up to check the time. Two in the morning. I've been lying here, wide awake, for over an hour. I carefully lay my head back, thinking about earlier. After he cleaned me up, he gave me one of his GCM tees and pulled me out into the kitchen to one of the stools at his breakfast bar. I watched as Keeton made us steak and eggs. Thank goodness, because I was starving since we really didn't finish dinner. After that, we ate the dessert (apple pie à la mode) out on his deck that overlooked his pool and land—lots of land. "How much of this is yours?" I asked once I'd had more than enough pie.

The moon was full enough to illuminate his property, so he pointed to his right and said, "From that tree line way over there," his arm swung left, "to that one over there."

"Wow, that's a big lot. So, this is all yours? You live here alone?"

"I do."

"Don't you ever get lonely?" I know I would. I need people around me, even if it's just a neighbor.

He pulled my hand, tugging me until I was on his lap. He brushed my hair away from my face and kissed my cheek. "I do. But you're here now. How can I be lonely with you here?"

I laughed. "I won't be here forever."

"Why not?" He smirked. "Plenty of room."

"Keeton." I laughed again and slapped his chest playfully. I mean, he couldn't be serious, right?

He kissed my neck and whispered in my ear, "Just think about it."

I froze on the spot. *Was he serious?* While my inner romantic wanted to jump up and down and yell, "Yes! Yes!

Yes!" at the top of my lungs, Lainie the realist knows this isn't a fairy tale. It's not real. It's too soon. *Waaaayyy* too soon. Relationships in the real world, the one I was just divorced in, don't happen this fast. While I wanted to ignore him, that would be taking the easy way out. I couldn't do that. If this was anything at all, I needed to be honest with him. I needed to explain.

Turning to look at him, I smiled. "I'm going to tell you a story and hope you'll listen to it from start to finish. Will you do that?"

He nodded.

I slid off his lap to sit across from him, because I couldn't think straight in that position. "I won't bore you with all of the details of my fake marriage, but I need to give you some backstory, so you know where I'm coming from. That okay?"

"Of course it's okay." He leaned forward in his seat, hands clasped together between his legs.

"First, the reason I married Lewis was because I didn't think I'd ever get married. I never thought anyone would ever ask me, so when he told me what he needed, I jumped at the chance. I figured I could live with him, finish school since I had one year of college under my belt, start a career, and we'd end things once he was more secure in his job."

I stood up and walked over to his railing. Turning to face him, I went on. "I was the first of my girlfriends to get married. Dad was happy for me but apprehensive, and my sisters thought I was the bomb." I laughed. "For once, I wasn't the ugly, fat one. I was the bride." Keeton made a growly noise, but I ignored it and continued. "The wedding was small." I rolled my eyes. "I guess they call it intimate. I wore a plain white dress I found at a discount plus-size store and carried a bouquet from the grocery store. My dad was confused, because I guess he thought his oldest daughter, and first to marry, should have a big wedding. I swear," I laughed again, "my dad thought I was knocked up." I laughed some more. "What a joke, right?"

Keeton stood and walked to stand next to me.

"I moved into the condo Lewis had just purchased, and that was it. I had my own room, which was good. But it wasn't easy. Living with Lewis was, at times, unbearable. He expected me to do *almost* everything a wife is supposed to do. He wanted me to clean, cook, look pretty," I said snidely. "He was always on me about my weight, what I wore, what I ate, and when I told him I was going to continue to work on my degree, he went ballistic."

"Why?" Keeton had reached out now, his hand on the arm I had resting on the railing.

I shrugged. "He liked it the way it was. I think he figured if I got a degree, I'd leave him as soon as I graduated."

"So, what'd you do?"

"I did what he asked me to do. Until I didn't." I chuckled. "I started to 'disobey' him," I said with air quotes. "I listened to him talking to his investment buddies and took notes. Then I started investing. I made enough in six months to start taking online classes. It took me almost four years to finish, but I earned my degree in English plus I continued to make money investing. Not a ton, but enough."

"I think I know what you're going to say now."

"Oh?"

"You're going to say you're not ready to be tied down again." He ran his thumb over my cheek, pushing my dark hair behind one ear. "That you want get to know yourself again."

"I know myself. I've always known myself, but I did get a little lost while I was married to him. Torn between my role as a wife and knowing it was all a sham. I was living some kind of weird alternate reality designed by Lewis."

"He divorced *you*? Why?"

"No idea." I shrugged. "His attorney showed up at the

condo with papers. I signed them. He told me I had fifteen days to vacate the premises, so I called an emergency meeting of the Palmer sisters. Keely offered me her spare room, which I gladly accepted and moved out the next weekend. I started writing the day after I unpacked."

"I know this isn't my business, but I need to ask. Why didn't you ask for anything in the divorce? He knew you didn't have a job, hadn't worked in ten years, and he left you nothing. That's not cool."

I placed my hand on his chest and rubbed gently. "I didn't want anything from him, Keeton. I was so relieved it was over. I've got a solid family behind me in every way. If I needed help, they would have given it to me. They were all so relieved I was out too. Privately, they all offered to help me financially. But I was okay with the portfolio I'd been nurturing for a while."

"So, now are you going to tell me it's too soon?"

I nodded and smiled. "It's too soon, Keeton. I'm not ready to move in with you. I like you, a lot. I want to see where this goes, but I need to take it slow to figure things out. I want to see if I can write a book."

"Alright. And for the record, I like you a lot too." He kissed me with fervor. "A lot, a lot."

Giggling, I nuzzled my head beneath his chin. "Good to know."

KEETON DROPPED me off at my apartment at the ass-crack of dawn. I'm a morning person but being woken up at five in the morning to be kissed, licked, and loved has given morning person a whole new meaning. As quietly as possible, I unlock the door to our apartment. Shutting it behind me, I step into our small galley kitchen and start a pot of coffee, then go to the refrigerator and pull out the cream, along with a container of yogurt. "Healthy," I mumble to myself. "Rather have a donut." But that's not smart.

As I stand waiting for the coffee to brew, I close my eyes and think about, well, everything. The sex, in particular. This morning he was gentle and slow, like he was making love to me rather than just having sex. I know, you don't have to say it. I'm just imagining that things with Keeton are real and forever. I know it's preposterous, but it's fine. I'm a writer; I'm allowed some creative license.

Coffee finally brewed, I pour some of the nectar of life into my favorite mug. It was my mom's from way back when—it's blue on the outside and yellow inside. There are flowers that look like they're growing up from the bottom of the cup and the words World's Best Mom running along the top edge. I gave her the cup for Mother's Day one year. I remember picking it out. I thought it was almost as pretty as she was. So, yeah, Dad thought it was fitting I should have it. A hot tear reaches the corner of my eye, and I shake it off. "Not this morning, Lainie. This is going to be a great day."

Stepping past our small dining area—Keely calls it a niche—I start to go into the living area when I hear a knock on my front door. A chill runs through me, thinking of Keeton coming by because he can't stop thinking about me. "You live in a fantasy world," I mutter to myself.

At the door, I look through the peephole and freeze. "Lewis? What are you doing here?"

"Open the door, Lainie. We need to talk."

No, we don't. "I need to get ready for work."

"That's one reason I'm here. Please open the door. Just for a minute."

Resigned, I open the door and step out onto the walkway. "What?" I say with hands on my hips.

"I'm concerned about you, Elaine."

"Lainie."

"Lainie." He rolls his eyes. "I'm very concerned."

"There's no reason for concern. I'm fine."

"But you're working for a mechanic. A grease-monkey, for Christ's sake, Lainie."

I scoff. "He's not a grease—"

"Do *not* interrupt me, young lady."

Young lady? We're the same age, practically. He's a few years older. Not old enough for this crap.

"Where were you last night?"

"Uh, what?"

"I asked where were you last night."

"That's none of your business, Lewis."

"Of course it's my business. You're my wife."

"*Ex*-wife."

"You still represent me. You can't start whoring around town and expect it not to come back on me."

"Whoring around?" I squeak.

"What else can I assume? You were gone all night."

How does he know this? "Have you been sitting outside my apartment or something?" I know he couldn't be tracking me anymore. I deleted the app.

"It doesn't matter how I know." He steps closer to me, and I move back until I bump into my door. In a sugary sweet voice, he says, "I'm worried about you. I think you're setting yourself up for heartbreak."

"H-heartbreak?"

Lewis chuckles, and it's creepy. "You can't expect a man like *that* to want someone who looks like you," he says, looking me up and down. "He's using you, Lainie. Hell, I suspect he'll dump you the minute he gets what he wants."

My eyes grow round.

"Oh, I see. He's already fucked you? Wow, either he works fast or you're desperate."

"Lewis. Go home," I say angrily. I feel the burn of tears but squeeze my eyes shut to stop them.

"Oh, honey," he coos. "You seriously think a man like that would want *you?* I've seen his picture. He's hot. He could have anyone. *Anyone,* sweetie. He's not going to want the fat girl for more than a night or two. After that, he can tell his buddies about it, so they can laugh."

Why is he saying this? I was always nice to him. I took care of him and He. Divorced. *Me.* Not the other way around. Turning the handle, I push the door open with my butt. As soon as I'm inside, I slam the door shut and let the tears fall.

The shower calms me, settles me. It also gives me time to think about the night before. "Lewis, you jerk, you're wrong." I know Keeton isn't using me. And why is Lewis suddenly so interested in my life? He never cared before. Heck, he only noticed me when he needed something. Then, I was worth his time. "Yeah, Lewis. You're a jerk."

CHAPTER NINETEEN

KEETON

AFTER DROPPING LAINIE OFF, I race home to shower. Halfway home I regret not showering quick before taking her home because I could have showered *with* her. Now I'm back on my bike and to work before eight. I haven't been this early in months. I usually hang out at home, work on some drawings, drink coffee, and relax. But not today. Nope, I want to be here when Lainie arrives. Plus, I've got a shit-ton of work to catch up on. But, mostly it's to see Lainie walk in the door. I want to see that blush she'll get when she first sees me. That'll tell me she's remembering last night. And this morning.

I get right to work checking messages. In retrospect, doing that first was a bad decision. The first voice I hear is a former customer. Former because I never plan on doing any work for him again. Ever. Six months ago, he sued me over damage that *he* caused to his own bike because he was drinking and driving. He blamed it on mechanical error rather than on the bourbon he drank at the bar. Luckily, the cops gave him a breathalyzer test at the scene. They saved my ass. I chuckle. That's the one and only time I'd ever say a cop did anything but *ride* my ass.

I replay the message, and the good mood I had when I walked in is long gone. The fucker is seriously asking me to settle? He lost. The case is closed, or the judge threw it out, so that's closed, right? I continue to listen.

"Mr. Gustafson, I wanted to give you the opportunity to settle with me before I take my case to the next level."

The next level? What the fuck is the next level?

The asshole keeps right on talking. "I've retained new counsel who assures me he has an expert mechanic who looked the bike over and noticed some glaring mechanical issues."

"Yeah, *now* it's got mechanical issues, you fucking cocksucker. You totaled it," I growl, knowing he can't hear me.

"My attorney will be in touch."

I hear the phone click and stare at my answering machine. I want to pick it up and throw it through a goddamn window, but I don't. Instead, I stomp to my door just as Lainie appears. "Oh, hey, Keeton."

I'm too pissed to enjoy seeing her like I'd planned. She doesn't need to see me like this either. "Not now, Lainie," I say loudly. Dammit, she deserves nice Keeton. Not this guy. I stomp past her, through the showroom, and out the door. I hope to fuck the day gets better.

It doesn't. I think it gets worse. For one, the parts I ordered weeks ago still aren't in. When I called the company, I did my best to hold my foul mood back, but I wasn't successful. So, instead of finding out when I'd get my shit, I get the sound of the phone being slammed down in my ear. With that not sorted out, I get to work slamming my thumb into the drawer of one of my rolling toolboxes, slipped in some grease the crew didn't get cleaned up, and on top everything else, Eric's nowhere to be found.

"Where the fuck is Eric?" I yell from the doorway between the shops.

Billy is the poor sap that's closest. "Twenty-four-hour bug?"

Bullshit. "Are you asking me or telling me?" I squeeze my hands into fists to keep my anger to myself. "He's either hungover or he's got pussy in his bed." Bill shrugs, and I growl. "Call him and get his ass in here, Bill. Now!"

Before I stomp back to work, I see pink. Lainie is standing fifteen feet from me, clutching papers to her chest. Her eyes are big as saucers. She's probably got a question, but I'm not ready to talk to her. I'm only going to be grouchy, and paperwork can wait. "Not now, Lainie. I've got more important shit to do." I don't wait for her to respond. Turning on my heel, I stomp back to my side of the shop and get back to work.

By lunch, I've calmed the fuck down. I get into a groove working on the new bike design. Creating always calms me. Now that I've had a few hours, I think I can finally talk to Lainie, give her the nice Keeton. I walk to her office but it's empty. Checking my watch, I note the time. Noon. I peek in my office, stop at the bathroom, and then back out to the shop where, lo and behold, my fucking brother is.

"Where's Lainie?"

He glares at me, then coughs. His voice sounds scratchy when he says, "Lunch. With Molly."

Oh, right. Molly was coming by. "Why didn't she come back and say hi?"

"Probably because you were in one of your fucking snits." He coughs again, and it's deep. It sounds painful.

"What's wrong? You sick?"

"Jesus, asshole. Yes. I called in sick. It's what you do when you're sick."

"Go home." I shrug. "Before you infect the rest of the crew."

"Fuck!" Eric shouts at the ceiling. "You're a goddamn menace, you know that? I'm out. And I'll be late tomorrow." He stops in front of me. "If I come in at all."

"Sure. Fine. Go take care of you."

"Fucker," he mumbles as he leaves.

"Jesus. What bug crawled up his ass?" I look up at Billy, who's staring back at me. "What?"

"Nothing, boss."

Seriously, what the fuck?

WIPING MY HANDS, I stare down at the motor I just built. I won't know if it runs until I've got the rest of the parts and everything's together, but it looks good. I feel like I accomplished something today. Stopping at the sink, I use thick hand soap to clean the stuff off my skin. I don't want to get anything on my girl when I wrap her up in my arms.

At her office door, I stare at darkness. Her light's off, and it's only three-thirty. Did she say she had to leave early today? I can't remember her mentioning it. I pull the phone out of my pocket to see if she sent me any messages, but there's nothing new. Back out in the shop, I see Billy knee-deep in the blue Honda. "Billy. You see Lainie leave?"

Without looking up, he replies, "Nah, boss. I think I saw her and Molly together, but not sure."

I bet she and Molly are off doing girly shit. The thought makes me smile. I love imagining Molly smiling and that my favorite sister is with my favorite girl. I won't bother 'em. This is good for both of them. I lean over the hood of the blue piece of shit. "So? Thoughts?"

"About Lainie or this car?" Billy still hasn't looked up, but if you can hear a smirk, I heard it.

I'm tempted to say "both," but I really don't want to hear what Billy has to say about Lainie. I'm sure it'd be something that'll piss me the hell off. Now that I'm finally in a better mood, I'd prefer to keep it that way. "The car."

Pulling his head up, he straightens his arms so his body's no longer lying over the front end. "This is a pointless endeavor."

Endeavor? When did Billy get a vocabulary?

"That's what I figured." Now what do I do? "Can we part it out?"

Billy arches a brow. "Yeah, but it's going to be worth less than five hundred."

"Good enough. I'll talk to Lainie. Tell you tomorrow. Thanks for trying. Head out early if you want."

"I want. Thanks, boss."

Back in my office, I stare down at my answering machine as it blinks. I know if I listen, there's a about a hundred percent chance it's going to piss me off. But it's Friday. I've gotta listen. Pressing the button, it tells me I have one new message.

"Keeton. This is Mitch. Just got a call from an attorney representing—"

I hit delete and call him direct. No use to hearing this shit twice.

"Keeton. You got my message?"

"Yeah. What's happening? I got a message from the prick this morning. Says he's got new evidence."

"He did? That's not appropriate, for him to call you."

"Whatever. What'd his lawyer say?"

"That they have an expert who can corroborate the theory the bike was mechanically flawed."

"Bullshit, Mitch. How's he gonna know that after it was totaled?"

"He can't. I know who his 'expert,' is and he's a clown. I'll file a motion to have our own expert look the bike over."

"Should I be worried?"

"No way. I've got this."

"Fine. Keep me updated." I hang up and run my hand over my practically bald head. I miss my hair. I miss my girl more. But I'll give the girls time to do their thing.

At home, I shower then flop my ass on the couch, flipping on the television, I look for a game to watch. I find some baseball and close my eyes.

When I wake, my dick is as hard as a rock in my loose shorts, and I blink, trying to figure out where I am and if, in fact, Lainie just gave me the best blow job of my life. Shaking my head, I realize it was just a dream. A fucking hot as hell dream. When I check the time, I see it's just past eight. *How long was I asleep?* Enough time to have the dirtiest dream imaginable. Picking up my phone, I decide to text her. Maybe she'll come over and really do the shit I just dreamed about.

Me: *Hey, babe. Wanna come over?*

CHAPTER TWENTY

Lainie

HOLDING my phone in my hand, I stare at his message.

Keeton: *Hey, babe. Wanna come over?*

"Who's that from, or do I even need to ask?" says Keely, reading over my shoulder. "Ooh, that's a booty call. You gonna go?" She smirks.

It's Keely's unique way of encouraging me, I suppose. But she doesn't know about today—about Lewis's visit or about Keeton's harsh brushoffs. I left early because I was barely holding it together at the shop. I *am* only the temp, and Molly told me I was doing a great job—that I was up-to-date on everything. And I told Keeton when I took the job that it needed to be flexible. So why shouldn't I leave? I didn't feel it was necessary or prudent for me to approach Keeton again. I can take a hint.

The part that hurts the most is the fact that Lewis was right.

Keeton was, or is, from the looks of the text, just using me. He wants sex. All of that bull he said last night was just that, bull. Lies. I don't know why he had to do it. I mean, I was already there in his bed willing to do whatever whorish things he wanted to do to me. "God, I'm such an idiot."

"Why do you say that?"

"No reason," I mumble. I wish I hadn't said that out loud. I'm not ready to admit how stupid I am. I'm the oldest, Keely's the youngest. I should know better. I need to teach by example and if she sees how easily I fell into his bed and how badly it hurts to be used like this, I won't be able to look her in the eye again. Besides, she won't be able to keep it to herself. She'll blab to the rest of the girls and I can't face it. I'm not strong enough yet.

"You should totally go over there. You had fun last night, right?"

"Sure." Yes, I had a great time. But I'm not like Keely. I can't just hook up with a guy and laugh it off like she does sometimes.

"Then go." She reaches for my phone, but I'm fast enough to pull it away.

"I've got this. Now get back to doing whatever it is you're doing." What *is* she doing? "What are you doing?"

"I'm just making some notes to prepare."

"Prepare? For what?"

"My court battle."

I stand with my mouth agape. Speaking extra slow, I ask, "Court battle?"

Rolling her eyes and sighing like she thinks I'm the dumbest person, she responds, "My appeal."

"Appeal?"

"Yeah."

"For what?"

"Oh, just a speeding ticket."

I look at the rectangular piece of paper sitting on the table in front of her and blink. "Again?"

"Yeah. Geesh." Keely rolls her eyes. "Nothing to worry about, sis."

"Uh-huh."

She looks down at her notes, then back up at me. "Lainie, I'm innocent."

"Uh-huh. So, you're appealing the ticket?"

"Oh, yeah." She nods. "It was entrapment."

"Right." Note to self: Call a family meeting. Topic? Keely's lead foot. "Wait! You didn't get a ticket in Keeton's car, did you?"

"Not yet." She winks. "But, there's still time."

No, there isn't. I plan on returning Keeton's car as soon as possible. "You won't have time. Our car is going to be done soon."

"Well, that's a damn shame, sis. That's a sweet-ass ride."

It sure is. "When I buy a car, I'll try to get something halfway nice." I should make a note to myself to get that done this week.

I walk into my bedroom and lie down on my bed. Staring at the phone, I think about my reply. I'm definitely not going over there but I don't want any drama.

Me: *Can't. Busy.*

I only have to wait a few seconds.

Keeton: *I miss you. I want you in my bed.*

And there it is. Stupid Lewis.

Me: *Can't, sorry.*

Me: *What's the update on my sister's car?*

I wait. It takes him longer than a second this time.

Keeton: *We're going to sell it for parts.*

What in the heck? Why does that instantly make me angry? Who does this guy think he is? It's not his car, which means it's not his decision to make. I'm getting pretty tired of having people in my life, men, to be specific, who think they know what's best for me without ever asking me what's best for me.

Me: *Uh, what!? No. We need the car back. Keely can't afford to just go out and buy a new car. Besides, that's not your place to decide. It's Keely's car.*
Keeton: *Babe. It's in bad shape.*
Me: *Keeton. I want the car back.*
Keeton: *I was going to get you something else with the money.*

Again. He's overstepping.

Me: *We love that car. It has history. We want it back.*
Keeton: *Fine. I'll get Billy to put it all back together. You can get it later this week.*
Me: *Fine. Thank you.*

I set the phone down and decide to hunt down some candy. I need something sweet to eat. Back on my bed, I see his reply.

Keeton: *So, you don't want to come over?*
Me: *No.*
Keeton: *You pissed at me, babe?*

Me: *No*

Yes. But, I'm not about to rock the boat. I hate drama that can be avoided by simply keeping my mouth shut.

Keeton: *Alright. Sweet dreams, beautiful. See you in the morning.*

I don't reply. My emotions are all over the board. I'm upset with him—angry about the car and sad about him using me and mad at myself for being too stupid to know it. "God, men suck."

"Word," mutters my sister as she passes by my bedroom door.

It makes me laugh. Hard. My sisters are the best. Why do I need a guy when I've got them?

Okay, don't answer that. I know why. At least after last night I do, but I've got a drawer full of boyfriends. I'll be fine.

ASK me how much sleep I got last night. Alright, I'll just tell you. None. Zero. Zilch. I tossed and turned all night thanks to my day yesterday. I kept hearing Lewis's voice in my head and then I remembered the way Keeton blew me off yesterday, and that memory made me cry. Long story short—it made for a very rough night. By the time my alarm beeps loudly, I've made one decision. I'm calling in, or in my case, texting in sick.

Me: *I'm not feeling well. I won't be in today.*
Keeton: *Must be going around. Eric's got it too.*

I'm sure Eric doesn't have what I have, but I keep that to myself.

Keeton: *Feel better, baby. Want me to bring you anything?*

He's probably just referring to his penis. But he could also be talking about medicine or chicken soup. Who can tell?

Me: *No, Keely's here.*

He doesn't need to know Keely's teaching during the day. Keeton doesn't reply, and I'm okay with that.

Confession. By eleven in the morning, I was no longer okay with it. I'm not okay with shirking my duty at my temporary job even though the last thing I want to do is face Keeton. But, face him, I must. I will also tell him that this will be my last week. My first week will be my last week. That's not going to look good on a résumé. It can't be helped, though. Besides, I need to return the car. I don't feel right driving it any longer. I know Keely would like to drive it forever, but she knows that's not going to happen.

I shower and dress in jeans and a pretty, flowy top. I also wear my favorite pink Mary Janes. They always give my spirit a lift, as well as my height, *ba-dump-bump*. By noon I'm in the back parking lot and staring at the back entrance to GCM. "Open the dang car door, Lainie. You. Can. Do. It." I recall saying something similar less than a week ago.

This door doesn't squeak like the old car door. Instead it chimes something pretty, reminding me to take the key fob with me. I grasp it in my right hand, shut the door, and make my way inside. I hold the door so it doesn't slam shut. I'd rather not alert anyone I'm here just yet. I still need to gather my courage. Plus, I need to push my shoulders back and hold my head high. In my brain, I say positive things like: *You did nothing wrong, Lainie. You took a risk, you did some naughty things with a big, sexy biker man. You should be proud of yourself for taking the risk.* Right?

As I move into the hallway that leads to the offices, I hear raised voices. Angry voices. Should I go back out? I don't feel it's my place to eavesdrop on a private conversation, especially one that sounds as heated as this one. That's when I recognize one of the voices. Lewis. "What is Lewis doing here?" I whisper to myself. I used the back driveway. If I'd pulled up front, I might have noticed his car. I move to the wall and slowly scoot closer to Keeton's door. I don't want either man to know I'm listening.

"Why are you here, man?"

That was Keeton.

"You know why I'm here."

"No, I don't."

"I'm concerned about Lainie."

"Concerned?"

"She seems to be making some very bad choices of late."

Keeton chuckles. "Bad choices? What is she, ten?"

"If the shoe fits," Lewis adds smugly.

"She's got a new life, man."

"A new life?" he squawks. "She doesn't need a new life. Her life with me was perfect."

I scoff to myself. *Perfect?* Is that guy mental?

"I beg to differ," says Keeton, sounding calm and collected.

"Beg all you want, but Lainie belongs with *me*."

Then why did you divorce me asshole?

"Lainie's life is none of your business anymore."

"None of my business?" Lewis's voice went up an octave. "She's my *wife*."

Keeton laughs, but it's humorless. "Ex-wife. And from what I hear, you weren't much of a husband in the first place."

"That's none of your—"

Keeton doesn't let him finish. "You treated her like shit,

dude. A woman like Lainie deserves to be treated with respect and worshipped, like a queen."

Lewis returns with his own humorless laugh. "You're not good enough for her. You're not good enough to shine her shoes. She belongs with *me*."

Okay, there's so many things wrong with that statement. First, what!? I can't believe Lewis would say something like that. All I ever heard was what a useless waste of space I was from him. Second, shine my shoes? Do people still do that? No matter, the fact that he's claiming I'm his is starting to get on my nerves. It's too late to attempt to make amends now. I let him mess with my head for ten years—I'm not doing that anymore. I lean in to listen again.

"I know I'm not good enough for her. But that isn't going to stop me. The second she stepped into my office, I *knew*." Keeton says the last word in a sexy, growly way.

"Knew what? That she was easy prey for a guy like you? She's not the brightest bulb in the lamp, you know."

"What the fuck are you talking about? She's smart as hell. You were married to her for ten years and you think she's dumb?"

He's defending me. And he's right. Lewis never really knew me.

"Look. She may be book smart, but when it comes to real life, to knowing about men like you, she's as naïve as they come. Hell, she actually believes you've got feelings for her." He snorts in disgust.

"I do. I'm in love with her and—"

He's in love with me? What!?

Scoffing, Lewis snaps, "In love with her? How long have you known her? A week?" He stops talking for a second, but then says, "Wait! Were you fucking her while we were married?"

"No, asshole. I just met her, but it only took one look."

Footsteps sound like they're getting closer to the door. I hesitate, not knowing if I should hide. I choose to stop and listen.

"You honestly think Lainie would ever cheat? Even with the arrangement you two had?" There's a pause, but Keeton adds, "I heard *you* cheated though."

Lewis chooses to ignore that argument, apparently. "You and I both know you're not what she needs."

"If you think she belongs with you, why'd you divorce her? *And* leave her nothing?"

"I did it because...." Lewis falters.

"Yeah, why did you do it, Lewis?" I whisper.

"I did it because...."

There's silence in the room. I'm holding my breath waiting to hear the answer.

"Yeah? Why?"

"Because. I wanted her to need me. She was pulling away. She got a goddamn college degree without my knowledge or approval. She started investing *my* money without *my* permission."

"Permission? Approval? This isn't the fifties, asshole. You think she had to ask permission to improve her own life? You're a dick, man. The woman is smart as shit. Sounds like she outsmarted you, anyway."

"Ha!" He makes a scoffing noise. "She'll do the same to you—take your money and use it to her own ends and then she'll leave you to whore around with someone new."

What!?

"Listen, fucker, she's not a whore and she's not the kind of girl that uses people. She's the kind of girl who does a guy a favor for ten fucking years, and what does that fucker do? He tracks her like she's a felon. Like a dog."

"I'm not tracking her, I—"

"I found the app on her phone," Keeton deadpans.

"I don't know what you're talking about."

That makes me think, how *did* Lewis know I was gone all night the other night? How did he know I was home the next morning? And he's here now. On a day I stayed home. "No," I say with a gasp. He can't still be tracking me. I deleted the app. I reach into my purse and pull out my phone. Sliding through my screens, I spot the app again. "No!" I drop the phone on the floor like it's covered in the plague. The noise is enough to draw attention to me. I've bent to pick it back up when I see feet. How can shoes show so much about a man? Lewis is in pristine brown suede loafers with those tassel things, while Keeton is in boots that are rough-and-tumble, thick and masculine. Yeah, those belong to Keeton. The same man who just said he loves me. I look up at both men but focus on Lewis. "You're still tracking me?"

"No, I—"

"How? I deleted the app."

Keeton reaches out, palm up. I place the phone in his hand. I watch as he scrolls through the screens. Looking at Lewis, he asks, "You do this remotely?"

"Yes," Lewis replies sheepishly. He knows he's been caught.

"Why?" I ask. "Why would you do that when we were married, and especially, why now?"

"Because I didn't trust you."

"You didn't trust me?"

"No. I found out you were going to college."

"How?" I didn't tell him. I only confided in my family.

"I found a letter from ASU. It upset me. I thought you were happy."

Shaking my head, I think, *he found a letter?* I was very careful. He must have gone through my things. "So you started to track me?"

Giving me a slight nod, Lewis adds, "I needed to know what else you were lying to me about."

"Lewis. You could have asked me."

"You would have lied," Lewis scoffed.

"Maybe, but we'll never know. Lew, you wouldn't let me do *anything*. You were angry about the notion of me working. You talked me out of continuing my education. Heck, you didn't even want me to spend time with my sisters." Now I'm getting riled up.

Lewis glares at me. "Hey, I did that for your own good. Your sisters are a terrible influence."

Yep, I'm getting riled.

"I kept monitoring you for your own good. I knew you were going to your sister's bakery all the time. I can only imagine how many calories you ate while you were there."

"You were keeping track of what she ate?" asks Keeton, but he shouldn't be surprised. I told him as much the other day.

"Her weight was out of control."

Keeton looks at me, scanning down my body. "Her body is fucking amazing." His eyes are smoky and sexy. "Thank fuck for your sister's bakery, babe."

I blush, but turn back to Lewis. He and I stare at one another for several seconds. "Yeah, Lewis. Thank *eff* for Sadie's bakery." I arch a brow, daring him to say another word. "You want to know what's sad?" I don't wait for a response. "I only wanted you to be happy, Lewis. I married you so you could achieve your goals. We were friends, or so I thought. Even though you talked down to me and treated me like crap, I still wanted you to be happy. I hoped you'd meet the right person and you'd finally live the life you wanted. Instead, you tracked me? You monitored my life like I was doing something wrong?" I step closer to Keeton. "The thing is, Lewis, as stupid as this sounds, I still want you to be happy. I mean, is your job really more important than your happiness?"

"I was happy with you," he says, barely above a whisper.

That's not true. "You divorced me."

"I had to. Before you divorced me."

"I wanted out, sure. But I believed in the vows we took. For better or worse."

"But you just got the worse, didn't you, Lainie?" I'm shocked to hear those words coming out of Lewis's mouth. "I got the better." His head is hanging in shame. "I know I treated you like shit, Lainie. I consciously tried to keep you down. I said things that hurt you to keep you insecure."

"It worked."

"I know." He looks me in the eyes. "And I'm sorry."

I don't know if he's truly sorry, but I'll take it if he'll leave now. "I'd like you to go now. Let me live my life, Lewis. You need to do the same. Think about what I said and just try to be content, at least."

He steps around Keeton and goes down the hallway. I watch him walk away for a second, but then look up at my big motorcycle hottie. "You love me?"

Chuckling, he says, "You heard that?"

"I did."

Nodding, he keeps smiling. "Good." He moves closer, until he's only a breath away. "Yeah, babe. I do."

Oh, my goodness. Keeton Gustafson loves me.

CHAPTER TWENTY-ONE

KEETON

I WRAP my arms around her and pull her to me.

"But we just met."

"So? There aren't rules about this kind of thing. The second I saw you, I knew."

She stares into my eyes. "I know. I felt that way too, but I just figured it was because you're so hot. I assumed everyone falls in love with you at first sight."

I chuckle. "I highly doubt that, love. But if that's the case, I've only loved one woman back." Kissing the tip of her nose, I add, "You, my beautiful Lainie."

She pulls out of my arms, stepping away, too far for me to draw her back. "You were so mean to me yesterday. I thought it was your way of pushing me away. I assumed you decided one night was enough." She rolls her eyes. "Until the booty call."

"Booty call?"

Jamming her hands on her hips, she snaps, "Keely said it was a booty call. I'm not a booty call kind of girl, Keeton."

"Well aware, dollface. You're the real deal."

"I am. I'm a keeper."

"I know, honey. That's—"

"But, I'm not sure I'm ready for all of this right now," she says, waving her hand around in a circle. "You're pretty intense, Keeton."

I squeeze my eyes shut. I am that. "I know."

"Keeton. I just got out of a terrible marriage. I was looking forward to spending time writing."

"I know."

"I can't just assume we're a sure thing. What if I don't like you in a month or two?"

"It's possible." I smirk. "I am an asshole."

She makes a frustrated noise. "I hear that."

"So, what now?" I ask, sitting down in my office chair. I'm giving her space so she has a chance to say what's on her mind.

"I think we should date."

"Date. Okay." I'm all for dates, especially if they end up like our first one.

"I'll work here until Molly gets back, but I am not going to be here all day. I want to write, and I do my best work in the morning. So that means I won't be in until lunchtime."

"Fine. But may I make a suggestion?"

She doesn't answer right away. If I had to guess, I'd say she was preparing for me to suggest she not write or something.

"What is your *suggestion*?" She says it like it's something distasteful.

"I've got an empty office here. We could turn that into your writing room."

She looks up at the ceiling, then back to me. She's considering it. "Can I see it?"

"Sure." I stand up and grab my keys. "It's next door." Stepping up to her, I take her hand in mine and lead her to the next office. "It's small," I warn her before I open the door. "But it's the only one with a window."

"Oh?"

Unlocking the door, I look back at her. "I keep this locked because I store my designs in here but I'll move those out of here so you can have the whole office."

"I see," she says as I push the door open. Inside is a desk, a chair, a small bookcase, and a filing cabinet. There's not much room for anything else. "Keeton. It's perfect." Smiling, she moves to sit in the chair. "Why don't you use it?"

"We'd set it up for Eric to use but he hates the idea of being cooped up in an office, so it sits empty." The room is dusty as hell. "All it needs is a good cleaning and a fresh coat of paint." I move to sit on the corner of the desk, looking down at her as she opens desk drawers. Then she stands to peer out the small window, she opens the blinds to see beautiful Arizona sunshine flood the room, making Lainie smile. "So? What do you think? You can work in here in the morning, then move to Molly's office in the afternoon. When Molly comes back, you can write full-time."

"Would I have to answer the phones in the morning?"

"Nah, one of us will get it or it'll go to the machine." Standing, I turn toward the door. "Hang on, I've got another computer and an extra printer we can put in here."

Following me out the door, she says, "Working at Keely's tiny kitchen table is for the birds, but it's better than feeling like I owe you something. It all sounds too good to be true."

I stop and turn to her. "Why?"

"Because," she flutters her long lashes at me, "what's the catch?"

I'm close enough to touch her, so I do. Moving a silky curl

out of her face and pushing it behind her ear, I stare at her pretty face. There's real concern in her eyes. After meeting Lewis, I think I know where that's coming from. "Lainie, I get why you're apprehensive about me, about this office, about everything. I just met the reason a few minutes ago."

She gives me a tiny nod of her head.

"I'm going to be completely honest with you right now. All right?"

Another nod.

"I've never felt this way about anyone before. My biggest fear is that you'll walk out of here and I'll never see you again. So, yes, I'm offering you this office space for my own selfish reasons. I want you here with me during the day, and I'm hoping I'll have you in my bed at night too."

"Not every night," she says quickly.

I chuckle, but it's a nervous laugh coming from a very insecure place. One I had no idea lay dormant. "I'll take what I can get with you."

Lainie puts her hand on my chest, right above my heart. I love her hands on me. "This is all very confusing for me, Keeton. I just need time to process it. What if we get sick of each other?"

I chuckle. "I don't think I'll get sick of you." Ever. "But if we do? Then we talk about it."

"Can I sleep on it?"

"As long as it's at my place, sure."

"Can't. I promised Keely we'd watch Netflix tonight." She kisses me softly, then steps back. "Oh, and we want our car back."

"Babe?" I whine like a little bitch. "Just drive the loaner."

"Nope. I'll buy my own car. Keely needs her Honda back."

"Billy's tuning it up." Which is code for fixing whatever he can. "It'll be ready middle of next week. In the meantime, drive my car, and I'll help you shop for a new one. I know some people who have decent used cars." Deb, for one.

"I'm sure you do." She stares at me. "I'm buying my own car." Then she adds, "With my own money."

"Agreed. But I get to help you find one that's mechanically sound and within your budget."

She looks at me warily. "Fine."

"Fine," I repeat. "Come on. Let's get something delivered for lunch. I'm starving. I'll take you somewhere nice tonight."

"Can't. It's Friday night. Keely and I always order pizza on Friday night."

I look at her, giving her my best sad eyes. "Can I come over too? I'll bring the pizza."

"You can come over, but the pizza is on us."

I give her my best smile. "Sweet. What time?"

"Seven."

"I'll be there." With fucking bells on.

AT SIX FORTY-FIVE, I pull up to Lainie's apartment complex. Turning off my bike, I throw my leg over the seat, stow my helmet, and grab the grocery bag that holds a bottle of white wine, a six-pack of Bud, and a small bouquet of flowers. I look down at my shirt and fuss with it until it looks less wrinkled. "Shit. I'm officially a pussy." I laugh out loud because I don't care. I've never been happier in my life.

I knock and wait. In seconds, the door is flung open by Keely.

With a slightly slurred voice, she says, "Well, hello there, big guy."

"Hi?"

"Come on in, handsome," she giggles. "Let me take the flowers."

I step inside and scan the tiny space. When my eyes reach the living area, I spy more women. Three more. All of them resemble Lainie in some way or another. None of them hold a candle to her, but they're okay-looking. They're all staring at me, and it's unnerving. I look down at the coffee table and see several open wine bottles. I know how to get the focus off me. Holding up the grocery bag, I say, "I brought wine."

"Awesome!" says one of them. A tall woman stands up and takes the bag from me. Pointing to somewhere behind me, she says, "Lainie's in her room."

Without another word, I turn on my heel, heading in the direction she pointed. "Lainie?"

"Back here," she yells from somewhere further in the apartment.

I walk down the hall slowly, listening for clues as to the whereabouts of my woman. Passing a bedroom, I see her standing near what I assume is her closet. "Hey?" I say as I enter and shut the door behind me. I step up to her and wrap my arms around her. My nose is in her hair. God, she smells so damn good, like a summer breeze. Inhaling her scent, I press in until I'm completely against her. "There's a whole lot of women out there."

Lainie turns in my arms. "Surprised? Those are my sisters. I sent Keely a text letting her know you were coming. She must have called them all. Is that okay?"

"I've no problem with it if you promise to hold my hand."

She giggles. "Scared of my siblings, are you?"

"Hell yes. I have a feeling if I don't pass muster, you're going to dump my ass."

She laughs again. "They're going to love you."

"Like you do?" Jesus. That's something a lovesick pussy would say. Guilty.

"Keeton, I'm not—"

"Shh, it's okay. I shouldn't have put you on the spot like that." I kiss her neck because she smells so good right there and she likes it. The little moan she releases is all I need. "Okay?"

"I think you'll like them."

"I'm sure I will." I kiss her below her left ear again, whispering, "You're the prettiest one." I put my mouth on her earlobe to nibble and suck.

"Oh, no you don't." She pulls out of my arms. "You can't do that to me. I have company, and the walls here are like tissue paper. Stand down, sexy man."

I laugh and lean in for a kiss. "Just one kiss?"

With her pretty brow arched, she says, "Just one?"

"For now." I lean in and take her mouth. My hands are all over her in seconds flat. I want her so badly, but I do my best to keep things PG.

Pulling out of my arms, she takes my hand in hers. "Come on. Let me introduce you to the Palmer sisters." She turns, "Some of whom may have over-imbibed."

"I met one of those."

"Agatha?"

"Keely."

"Oh, I think Agatha is too. She's going through a rough patch. Ordinarily, she's quite reserved. You get to see her in one of her rare drunk moments."

"Awesome."

Lainie laughs and pulls me out of her bedroom by my hand.

CHAPTER TWENTY-TWO

Lainie

"EVERYONE, THIS IS KEETON." I've pulled the poor man into a living room that's crowded with Palmer women.

"Hi, Keeton," they all say simultaneously, like this is some sort of twelve-step meeting.

"Hi, ladies," Keeton says, smiling.

Starting with Keely, I begin the introductions. "Keeton, you know Keely."

"Yup."

"She's the baby." I point to Violet. "Her twin, Violet."

"Twins?"

"We know. We look nothing alike," mutters Keely. "Violet got all the good stuff. Height, long legs, great hair, perfect teeth, etcetera, etcetera, etcetera."

That comment surprises me a little, and I think Violet's a bit shocked too, since Keely has traits that none of the rest of us do. Adorable traits.

"Thank you, Keels," says Violet, blushing.

I've got to keep going, but I'd love to ask what that was all about. Keely doesn't normally dispense compliments freely. "Next is my middle sister, Sadie."

"The bakery owner?"

"I am. Have you been?" Sadie asks Keeton.

"Unfortunately, no. I plan to though. I hear my girl likes your sweets."

"Ah, man, you fuckin' rock," says Keely as she starts drinking another glass of wine.

"Slow down, lush," mutters Sadie. A comment that makes Keely throw her head back and cackle.

Ignoring all of that, I keep on going. "And finally," I point like a game show hostess, "this is Agatha."

Keeton steps around the table, holding his hand out for her to shake. One by one, he does the same to the remaining sisters. When he gets to Keely, she refuses his hand, instead standing up on her coffee table, making them close to the same height, although Keeton's still taller. "I need a hug, big guy."

Uh-oh.

Hesitant, Keeton steps close to her and wraps his arms around her. Patting her back gently, he pulls away, saying, "Nice to meet all of you."

"That hug sucked," mutters Keely. "Just sayin'."

Keeton laughs but returns to my side. "Sorry," I whisper.

He kisses my forehead, whispering in response, "You've met Eric, right?"

I giggle and lay my head on his shoulder. He gets it.

"So," says a drunk Agatha. "You're in a gang?"

The room erupts in laughter as Keeton looks down at me, running his hand through his short hair.

"Aggie, no," I say softly. "He designs and builds custom motorcycles."

"Oh." She takes a big gulp from her glass. "Right."

MY GOSH, Keeton is just so wonderful. My sisters asked him a million questions, and he asked them some in return. The girls' questions were a little too personal if you ask me, but he answered them all even though I chastised my sisters for it. His questions for them were thoughtful, like he was really trying to get to know each of them as individuals. My heart swelled listening to them banter and laugh with each other. Keeton could keep up with them, no problem. Lewis never did any of that. He barely tolerated them one-on-one. Keely was the exception, but Lewis avoided any kind of Palmer family activities, saying we were too much all at once.

When the wine was gone, Violet drove Aggie and Sadie home. She was drinking only water again tonight. I'm not sure why. Violet loves her vino. No matter, I'll get to the bottom of all that is going on with Violet soon. Keely was beyond drunk, so I sent her to bed while Keeton and I picked up the wineglasses, bottles, and empty pizza boxes.

I've been sort of quiet since they all cleared out. I'm waiting for the other shoe to drop, as they say. This would be the time, when we were alone, that Lewis would let his anger out. He'd tell me how livid he was that I let my sisters do this or say that. Like I can control my sisters—or even want to. He'd tell me I ate too much pizza and drank too much wine. That he expected better from his *wife*. Then he'd either leave or stomp to his bedroom, slamming the door as he went.

"Lainie?"

"Yeah," I answer as I wash wineglasses, never looking up.

"I'm sorry."

I stop, remaining stock-still. Here it comes. He's leaving. He can't be with me because he hates my family.

"I'm sorry if I did something wrong." His voice is hoarse but soft. He sounds choked up. "But, sweetheart, you're going to have to talk to me—tell me what it was, because I'm a fucking idiot. Will you do that?"

Surprised, I spin around, sloshing water all over the counter. "What?" He can't be asking me that.

"You won't look at me, honey. I can tell you're angry. What'd I do wrong?"

Oh, my God. This man. *My* man. I rush to him, wrapping my arms around him and pulling him as close to me as humanly possible. "Nothing." I feel a hot tear escape. "You did nothing wrong. You were p-perfect." Sniffling, I add, "I was worried you were going to yell at me about them. They're, they're—"

"Cool." Keeton says in my ear. I feel his tense shoulders soften beneath my arms. "They're cool, Lainie. I get why you love spending time with them."

"You d-do?"

"I do. Never a dull moment with the Palmer girls. Right?"

I laugh through my tears. "No. I love them so, so much, Keeton. Lewis hated them." I pull back a little to look at him. "Except Keely. He liked her."

"That guy's a tool." Keeton wipes a tear from my cheek.

"I thought you were going to be so mad after they asked you so many personal questions."

"Never pissed. I was more worried I wouldn't pass the test."

"What test?"

"That was a test, honey. They were looking out for you. Seeing if I was good enough for their Lainie."

"No. They're just nosy," I say, almost as an afterthought. It's then that I realize he's right. They were quizzing him. It *was* a test.

Looking at me with the most serious expression I've seen to date, he asks, "Do you think I passed?"

Releasing a sigh of relief, I nod. "With flying colors." I wrap him back up. "If you liked my sisters, you're going to love my dad, Keeton. He's the best man in the entire world. He raised us like a boss after my mom died." The tears start again, but these are happy tears.

"He raised pretty amazing women. I've no doubt he's a special man."

Okay, that does it. I start to sob on his chest, and my man just holds me, running his palm up and down my back. No more words are spoken. What else can we say? I know, right then and there, I love him. My heart is so full of love for him, I half expect it to burst. I won't tell him yet—I'm not ready to say it out loud. I can show him, though. Pulling out of his arms, I take his hand and pull him with me to my bedroom so I can make love to my boyfriend.

"What about the paper-thin walls?" he asks with a smirk.

"Keely's out cold." I giggle. "And I've got a lock on my door."

"Awesome."

And it was. So, so awesome.

CHAPTER TWENTY-THREE

Lainie

One month later

I CAN'T BELIEVE how good my life is right now. I'm constantly pinching myself because I can't believe it's real. I mean, I've got it all, including the man of my dreams. A man I *love*. Yeah, I finally said the L-word. It took a few weeks. I don't know why it took me so long to say it, because now you can't shut me up about it. I say it multiple times a day. It never gets old because he says it right back, or sometimes he says it first. I love it when he says it first.

Keeton's a very determined man. You probably knew that, but when it comes to me and us, he's twice as dogged. He wants me to move in with him. I think he asks me once per day, at least. I can't do it, though. Not yet. I'm still getting my footing after everything with Lewis. The confrontation here at GCM helped me get the closure I didn't realize I needed—the unanswered questions answered. I'm also glad I had the chance to tell Lewis I only wanted him to be happy. I don't think he's taken my advice yet. He's still at the bank, as far as I know. One day he'll do it. Maybe he needs to meet his person first. Perhaps that will be the catalyst.

The other thing I need to do before we take the next step is finish my book. Keeton stayed true to his word about having me write in the little office next to his. It's quiet, and Keeton leaves me to my work, most days. On other days, however, he can be quite the distraction, especially after he's read one of my steamy love scenes. He has inspired a lot of particularly graphic sex scenes. I try to get him to read those passages at home, but there are times I need my man's input on the spot.

Thankfully, Molly's back part time now, so he rarely starts with the hanky-panky at the office. Molly decided to come back to work after I told her how much I wanted to write. I think she was relieved I didn't want to keep her job. Maddy spends most days with Adam's parents so Molly can work. I think it's good for both of them, as well as Adam's family. They're a great support for Molly, who is still struggling with the loss of Adam. Shoot. I always tear up when I think about that little family. Then, when I imagine losing Keeton, it really takes me over the edge. I just can't go there.

As for my family? My dad has really gotten into the biker lifestyle. He hangs out at the shop frequently. He's been helping Keeton with a new design, acting as his assistant. I think both men are enjoying the time together. It's like they're long-lost friends, or perhaps my dad is the father Keeton wishes he'd had. Either way, it warms my heart to see the two of them huddled together talking about motors.

My sisters are all busy too. I've barely seen any of them in the last month or so since I've been immersed in all things

Keeton, but I need to make a note to myself to find out how they're all doing. I know Sadie's planning a cruise with her boyfriend, Andrew. Keely's school year is winding down. With her summer off, she's got plans to hang with her friends, take some continuing education classes, and goodness knows what else. Aggie is doing better since we held a family intervention at her house a couple weeks ago. She wasn't handling this loss-of-job situation well at all. She's still unemployed. I overheard Violet say she's going to help her find another job. That's good for both of them. As for Violet? She's taking a class or two this summer, as well as working part-time at Sadie's bakery. Gosh, I miss my girls. It's my job as the oldest sibling to keep an eye on them. Mom would have wanted it that way.

"You about done, babe?"

I'm supposed to be finishing up my newest chapter, but I'm stuck. There's something I need to know about a man's, well, his penis, but I can't bring myself to ask Keeton. My face burns hot even thinking about asking him. I stare at him as he leans, with both hands above his head, on my office doorjamb. It makes his arms look amazing. His tee has pulled up to reveal a little bit of his stomach. My goodness, Keeton's stomach is so carved and sexy. I love running my tongue over his abdominals. Oh, shoot, I let my mind wander into the lustful category.

He steps into my office, shutting the door as he comes. "What're you thinkin' about, Lain?"

"Keeton." I warn. "Molly—"

"Left for the day."

Uh-oh. Holding my hand up to stop him from advancing, I go to a place I shouldn't go. "I need to ask you about your penis."

He stops in his tracks. For a split second I think he's appalled by my query, but I'm wrong. Very wrong. I watch his hand move down past his heavenly abs to his crotch. "Oh, yeah? You want to talk about my cock?"

Penis. Geesh. Clearing my throat, I lean back in my chair and cross my legs, feigning confidence. "Yes. Describe what happens when you get an erection in, um, your jeans."

"This for your book, babe, or for you? You want my big, hard, cock?"

I'm flabbergasted. "Keeton," I squeak. "Of course, it's for my b-book." I don't know why I'm still so shy around him. I think he just surprises me with the things he says. My eyes haven't left his pants area since he placed his hand there. I can't help it. It's mesmerizing. He's moved close enough for me to touch it, him, if I wanted to, but I don't.

"Watch." He moves his hand away from his pants to my cheek. He runs his thumb down the side of my face to my mouth, over my bottom lip, slipping it into my mouth. I suck on it. What? Don't judge. It's for research.

I watch his erection grow, and grow, and grow. It starts to tent his jeans, then it extends until I see it move down the inside of his leg. I reach out and run my hand over it, up and down.

"Sweetheart," he murmurs.

God, I love this man. I feel his penetrating gaze, so I look up to meet it. "You want me to keep doing this?"

"No." He pulls away just slightly. Unbuckling his belt, I stare at his hands as he unbuttons his jeans and hear the *zzzzip* sound of his fly as he pulls it down slowly.

I'm tempted to reach out to pull his jeans and boxers down, but instead I lean back in my chair again so I can watch. This man is fascinating. I can't get enough of him. We shouldn't do this in the office, but if Molly's gone....

I stand up from my chair, bending slightly so I can reach up under my skirt. Wiggling out of my panties, I let them fall to the floor, kicking them to the side. Keeton hasn't taken his eyes off me. I lift my skirt up until it's around my waist. Turning away from him, I lean forward, placing my hands on my desk. Arching my back, I look over my shoulder. "Well?"

"Well what?"

"Are you gonna fuck me or what?"

"Christ, woman," he growls. "You're going to be the death of me." Moving up behind me, he leans down close enough for our mouths to meet. In a slow, seductive kiss, he tells me everything I need to know. He loves me, he cherishes me, and he thinks I'm sexy. "You're such a contradiction, my sweet, sexy, girl." I feel him move his erection right where I want it.

"Oh?"

"You've been blushing since I walked in the door. You turned almost fluorescent pink as you pulled your skirt up. When you bent over, I could see you bite your bottom lip. So fucking sweet, angel." He thrusts inside of me until he's fully seated.

"Keeton," I whisper. "Don't stop."

"I. Won't. Ever. Stop." He's pumping into me with each of those words. "I'm going to come so deep and hard inside of you. I'm gonna put my baby in you."

"Oh, God," I moan. He's been saying things like that for weeks. Every time he's inside me, he tells me how much he wants children. Children with me. It almost always puts me over the edge. Today is no exception. Using his right hand, he brings it around to my front so he can circle his fingers over and around my clit. I push back into him, hard, chasing my own orgasm. "Keeton. I'm close."

"Good. Get there, Lain."

I lay my head on my desk and arch my back as I press back into him. "There. I'm there," I moan. "Good. So good when you're inside me." There's nothing, and I mean nothing, that feels better than an orgasm when Keeton's inside. I hang on to the desk as he continues to work. His fingers are working on me again, trying to pull another one out of me. It's easier once I've had one orgasm, something else I didn't know until Keeton. I can have lots of them with Keeton. I squeeze the edge of my desk with both hands and feel the second wave hit. "Yes," I hiss. "Fuck, yes." I feel his entire body up against mine as he comes inside. A small orgasm floods out of me just thinking about him and me and a baby. *Our* baby.

CHAPTER TWENTY-FOUR

KEETON

A couple months after that

TODAY IS A BIG DAY. Lainie is *finally* moving in with me. Even last night my girl was still hesitant, though she's essentially already been living here with me. But today it's official thanks to my ace in the hole, her dad, Rob. He and I've bonded recently. It started over a couple of beers and a tour of my shop, and now he's helping me with my newest custom job. He's handy as hell and pretty fucking creative too. The man knows his bikes. Apparently, he owned a Triumph Bonneville back in the day, before he got married. He sold it to pay for his honeymoon. Before I met Lainie, I'd probably scoff at the notion of selling my bike for a woman, let alone a honeymoon—but not anymore. Now I get it. I also get that Rob Palmer is exactly the man Lainie described that night at her place. Honestly, he's the kind of husband and father I hope to be for Lainie and our future children.

Our children. Damn, I can't wait. When Lainie told me she was on the pill that night I met her sisters, I was honest with her. I told her I wanted kids, I wanted them with her, and I wanted to start as soon as she was ready. It was a risk. I thought for sure she'd either throw me out or curl up in a ball and ignore me. She did neither. She drew me in for a long sexy kiss and told me she'd pictured our children the day she met me. "Me too," I said. "They're all dark-haired and beautiful."

"I saw three little blondes in my imagination."

"How 'bout two of each?"

"Well, since we can't plan what our kids will look like, we can decide on the number but let's wait until after we have one. I have a feeling parenthood is harder than it looks," she laughed.

Confession. I got so fucking hard when she said that last part—*wait until after we have one.* I thought, *Fuck. She wants it too.* Since then, she's stopped with the pill and we've been checking every month since.

I'm pulled from my thoughts when a large van pulls into my driveway. "She's here," I say loud enough for Eric to hear. He's lying on his ass on my sofa waiting for the Palmer women to show up. Rob insisted on doing this part of the move with the help of Lainie's sisters. He said it was "Symbolic. Like passing the torch." I wonder if he did the same thing when she married the asshole. I'd ask, but I don't want to know the answer. I step out onto my porch and down two steps to meet Lainie at the back of the van. I kiss her pretty nose. "You ready for this?"

"I am," she says excitedly. "If you're sure?"

"Never surer of anything in my life, Lain." I lean down and kiss her deep. Several throats clear at once.

"Sorry," I mumble. Ignoring their mutters, I open the van door and take the first thing I see, a lamp. A lamp I recall seeing in Keely's living room. An ugly-as-sin lamp. The shade looks ancient but normal; it's the rest of it that's hideous. The base is a seated, ceramic Siamese cat. The thing is chipped and scratched to the point it probably needs to either be tossed or sent to be repaired.

Keely pats my back. "Yeah, I know. It's ugly, but you're going to have to deal, big bro."

She's taken to calling me big brother. I like it. "And why's that?" I ask smugly.

"Because I love it," Lainie says as she takes the lamp from me.

"Told ya." Keely smirks. "Deal with it."

"Our mom had it in her room growing up," Violet adds as she passes me. "It was Lainie's gift on her 16th birthday."

"Got it." We'll put it in a place of prominence. Taking the next box from the back, I walk into the house and set it down in the dining room. I'd moved the table and chairs off to the side to make room earlier.

After Lainie's boxes are piled high, the group gathers in my living room, some sitting, some standing. "I've got food to grill and drinks on the deck if anyone wants to hang out for a while."

They all turn to look at Lainie. Are they waiting for her approval? "Oh, cool. Thanks, babe." She kisses my cheek. "You all wore your suits, right?"

They all nod and then, "Hell yeah!" yells Keely. "Pool party!"

Okay. I guess we're having a pool party. Looking at my girlfriend, I ask, "Should I call Molly?"

"Um," she says, looking bashful. "I already invited her and the baby. They'll be here shortly. Is this okay?" She points to her family. "I shouldn't have assumed it was okay."

Molly has met a couple of her sisters, but surprisingly, this is the first time Eric's met any of the Palmer women. He's met Rob at the shop, obviously. I think it's why he volunteered to help with the move. He wanted to see if he could woo a Palmer sister for himself. I've been keeping an eye on Eric, and I must say, I'm surprised. He's been uncharacteristically quiet since they got here. It's interesting. Looking back at my new roomie, I say, "This is your home now. You can throw a party if you want, and since it took me months to convince you to move in, I think a party is definitely in order."

"Phew," she says, wiping sweat from her forehead—real sweat. Northern Arizona is hot this time of year. "I took a risk. I'm glad it paid off." Walking into the throng, she announces, "Girls! Time to swim."

Keely fist pumps. "Yeah, we get to lounge in the pool while the men cook."

"Yo, Keet. I'm swimmin' with the girls. Someone's gotta protect 'em."

"From what?" Rolling my eyes, I look over at Rob, then back to Eric. "Who's going to protect them from you?"

"Har-dee-fucking-har-har, big brother." Eric pulls off his shirt directly in front of Keely and Violet.

Keely hoots and hollers, "Whoa, son. I bet those big arms would be great putting together my Ikea furniture." The room breaks into laughter while Eric looks a little surprised by Keely's catcall. I think he's met his match in cute little Keely Palmer.

My eyes turn to Violet, who is now a bright shade of pink. She's doing her best not to look at Eric's shirtless torso. I should warn him to be careful around Violet. She's quiet and introverted. A guy as boisterous and arrogant as Eric could ruin her for life. As I take my first step toward him, Eric talks softly to Violet, and then he places his hand on her back and leads her out the door to the deck. Hell. Maybe I don't have to worry.

"I guess that means we're cooking, son."

I turn to see Lainie's dad next to me. "Sure, Rob. Right after

I show you something. It's out here." I lead him into my garage through the door in the kitchen.

This is his first time at my place, our place, so when he sees the bikes in my garage, he gasps. "Wow, you've got quite a collection."

"I do. I'll need to cut back as soon as Lainie gets...." Shit, we're not supposed to mention us trying to get pregnant.

"Good. I'm glad your priorities are in order." He chuckles. "For the record, I can't wait for a grand baby."

"Shit. Don't tell her I told you, would ya?"

He arches a brow. "I won't tell her you fucked up and spilled, son."

I laugh, because I've never heard him cuss before. "Here." I point to something I've got covered up in the corner. I wait until he catches up to me and then I lift the cover.

"Shit. Are you kidding me?"

"Nope. It's a '70 Triumph Bonneville."

"A T120," Rob says with awe. "How long have you had this one?"

"A while. It's been sitting in the back of the garage at the shop waiting its turn. I got it as a trade for a modification on another bike."

Rob runs his fingers over the retooled leather seat and the cerulean blue gas tank. "What'd you have to do to get it looking like this?"

I listed the work we did on the bike, including the leather work, paint job, new motor, and some other parts that needed to be re-chromed.

"It's beautiful." Rob's hand runs over the bike like it's precious. "Can I take it for a spin later?"

"Anytime." I hand him the keys. "It's yours."

He blinks at me, and I swear his eyes get shiny. "What?" he sounds raspy.

"It's for you."

"No. I can't."

"Why not?"

"Why would you give me a bike?"

I step closer to him. "Rob, you're my soon-to-be father-in-law and more of a father than mine ever was. Not only that, you're going to be the future grandfather to my kids. Lainie's told me about all of your sacrifices after Rachel died. You're the best man she knows." And Lainie doesn't bullshit. "To me, the best man the woman I love knows deserves this bike."

"It's too much. It's got to be worth twenty grand."

I shrug. "It's probably worth that now, but I got it for a song and the work was a labor of love."

He looks at me. "Seriously?" His eyes move back at the vintage bike. "You sure?"

"Positive. You just need to get it registered and insured. I've got it insured now if you want to ride it home today."

"Christ, Keeton. I'm not sure I can put into words what this means to me."

"No words needed. Just say you'll let me marry your daughter."

"Oh." He chuckles. "Is this a bribe?"

"No way. But if it helps...." I shrug.

"You have my permission, son. I've never seen my beautiful girl happier than she is with you. Just keep that up. If you don't, I'll kick your ass."

My turn to laugh. "Noted, sir."

"Does Lainie know you did this? That you're giving me this motorcycle?"

"Yep. She chose the color of the tank."

"Blue," Rob says softly. "Rachel's and my favorite color. Our wedding color—" His eyes are getting misty again. "Wow. No words, son. No words."

"None needed. Just have some fun. You've earned it. Come ride with me and the guys sometime."

Rob's eyes brighten. "Shit. I'd love that."

"Good. I'll put you on the contact list when we get a ride going."

"Wonderful."

"Let's go grill. I'm starving," I say, patting Rob's back.

"Good." He's still staring at his new wheels. "Good."

He follows me into the kitchen, where Lainie is waiting, fidgeting. "Did you like it, Dad?"

"Oh, sweetheart." He sniffles. "I love it. Thank you."

"It's all Keeton." She smiles up at me.

"The blue though. That was you. So thoughtful." Rob kisses Lainie's cheek and gives her a long hug. They're whispering to one another, so I step away to give them their moment. When they're done, Lainie's eyes are red, but her smile is just like the one I saw the first day in my office.

I'm in awe of her. "God, I love you so much, Lainie." I can't wait any longer. I was trying to make this thing special—do this out by the pool with everyone standing by, but I can't wait. I have to know. I step in front of her and kneel. I hear the door open to the deck, but I ignore it. My focus is on her. I reach into my pocket and pull out the ring I've been carrying with me for two weeks now. Holding it up in front of her, I try to speak but my throat is dry. Shit. I had the whole thing worked out. Now I can't remember it, because the way she's looking at me is taking my breath away.

Clearing my throat, I try my best. "Lainie, I never believed in love at first sight. Not until you walked into my office. I knew at that moment that you were meant for me. You're my person."

Lainie gasps, but I continue. "I've never loved anyone like I love you. If you'll marry me, I promise to spend the rest of my life working my ass off to make you happy. Will you—" I pause to swallow. "—marry me?"

She's looking into my eyes. I don't even think she's glanced at the ring. I know she will eventually; it's big enough it can't be missed for long. "Keeton," she whispers. "Everything you just said is the same for me. You're my person too. You know that. I can't imagine my life without you. Yes. Yes, of course I'll marry you."

I stand up fast and pull her in my arms. There's clapping behind us, and I look up to see everyone is in attendance. Even Molly and Maddy made it in time for the proposal. I lean down and kiss her lips. "So, do you want this ring or what?"

Lainie laughs until she sees the ring for the first time. "Holy shit, Keeton. That thing is huge."

"That's what she said."

"Who said that?" I ask, chuckling. I search the group of onlookers and spot the culprit. Violet. She's blushing again just like her sister—a bright shade of magenta. "Violet? That you?" I probably looked as shocked as Lainie. I've gotten to know her sisters. They're each unique. And what I know about Violet is she rarely speaks. She's a watcher, an observer. Her saying something like that is out of character, but hilarious.

"Yup," she says, giving me a smirk.

"Nice," says Eric, nodding and winking at Violet.

I should give Violet a heads-up about my brother, but I've got important things to do right now. Ignoring that exchange, I look down at the ring as I slide it on Lainie's finger. "I designed it myself." The center diamond is two carats, with smaller stones placed on either side and pierced gold work intended to look like flowers. That kind of work is called filigree. I learned a lot working with the jeweler. "Do you like it?"

"I love it." Staring at the ring, she asks, "Those are daisies, aren't they?"

"They are. And it's rose gold because you know how much I like you pink."

She blushes a deep magenta at my double entendre. "Well, sexy talk aside, I love it." She gets up on her tiptoes to kiss my lips. Wrapping her arms around me, she whispers in my ear, "Good timing."

"Why is that?" I stroke her back as I stare into her eyes.

"Because..." She moves up closer to whisper in my ear, "I'm pregnant."

I turn to stone in shock, but only for about five seconds. I lift her off the ground and spin her around, shouting, "I'm going to be a dad!"

"And a husband!" she shouts almost as loud.

"And a husband!" Fuck yeah!

BOOKS BY KAYT MILLER

The Palmer Sisters

Lainie

Agatha

Sadie

Cortland

Keely

Violet

Molly

Standalones

The Art of the Game

The Virginia Chronicles

One of a Kind

The Portrait Painter

Game Changer

The Flynns

Out of the Blue

Mick'sology

Vested Interest

The Importance of Being Ernie with Bonus Book The Importance of Being Kennedy's

Quirky Girl

For a complete list of Kayt's books, visit:

Kayt's Website: www.kaytmiller.com

Or Kayt Miller on Amazon.com

ACKNOWLEDGMENTS

Thank you to Hot Tree Editing and Lindsay Smith for editing this book from start to finish.

And an extra special thank you to Becky at Hot Tree Promotions for your advice, expertise, and your positivity.

And for my beta readers.
Thank you so much for your time and feedback!

ABOUT THE AUTHOR

How did it all start? Well, I love reading and one day I was searching for a book. A book about a certain type of woman and a specific kind of man and I couldn't find it so, I wrote it. I called it Game Changer and it couldn't have been a more appropriate title. It changed my life in many ways. While my real job is teaching young people, my fun job is conjuring up characters and situations to write about.

My goal, as a writer, is to write stories that relate to all of us, to make readers laugh and maybe cry sometimes. I hope my readers can escape into a fantasy, one that's actually possible. Sure, some of the stories could be dubbed "Insta-love" stories but that's okay. I fell in love with my husband pretty damn fast and with my daughter the second I saw her. So, it's a thing, I swear.

Please Follow Me on these social media sites. Following on BookBub to learn about special book deals.

I love hearing from you!

facebook.com/authorkaytmiller

twitter.com/kaytmiller1

instagram.com/kaytmiller1

bookbub.com/profile/kayt-miller

COVER DESIGN

The Palmer Sisters Cover Designs
by
Colleen Galligan
galligancolleen@gmail.com

Colleen,
Thank you for all of your hard work
and creativity on the new covers!
I love them! KM

THANK YOU!

Thank you so much for reading Lainie and Keeton's story! When I start a story, it begins with an outline, notes, and lots of crazy thoughts running through my head. When I actually start writing, the characters take over, leading me through the story like they're holding my hand—guiding me. The process is exciting and cathartic. With that said, I hope you enjoy the story.

If you did, please go to my website, www.kaytmiller.com, and join my newsletter so you can be the first to know what's coming up next. And...

And remember...Please, leave a review!

Thank you!

SNEAK PEEK: AGATHA

A PALMER SISTERS NOVEL 2

Chapter 1

Agatha

When the phone on my desk rings, I look down at the caller ID and see the name Miriam Smith. Strange. Why is the head of Human Resources calling me? In the past, when HR called, it was usually Trent, and it was just to chat. *Wait! OMG! This is it!* I know why she's calling. I'm *finally* getting that promotion. Lord knows I've applied for enough of them. I've been here at Heart & Sole Shoes for a little over eight years. In that time, I've become a Certified Public Accountant, I've completed every class and seminar offered by HR, and I've attended every conference there is to make me the best accountant I can be. Now, all I can say is, *it's about darned time!* Shaking my shoulders out, I take in a deep breath and answer my phone, "Agatha Palmer."

"Agatha, would please meet us in conference room three?"

"Now?" Miriam sure didn't waste any time on small talk.

"Now."

Wow, that's strange. I guess they're anxious to get this done. "I'll be right there."

I lean down to check the time on my computer. Usually, this is the time of day I'd be heading down to the ground floor for my morning coffee. Well, not just usually—always is more like it. At precisely 10:30 every workday morning, I leave my desk and walk to the best coffee shop in the city, Java Jane's. I step in line, savoring the smells of freshly ground coffee while perusing the large, whimsical menu board on the wall above the counter. I read through each item that is painstakingly drawn with multi-colored pieces of chalk contemplating what to get. By the time it's my turn to order I say, "A large, white chocolate mocha steamer please." While I wait, I tell myself that *next time*, I'll order something different.

What can I say? I'm a creature of habit. My family calls me regimented, like I'm in the Army or something. I disagree. I like routine; I'm used to a routine, but I can be flexible too, when need-be. The truth is, they know my schedule as well as me, maybe better. They know not to call me at work at 10:30, noon, or 3:15. Sure, they can text me or call my cell, but they also know I keep my ringer off while I'm at work. My focus is on my job. Period. They're also aware I go to bed at eleven every night except Saturdays. Yes, it's routine, regimented, but I find comfort in that.

Standing up from my desk, I exhale to calm my nerves. I look down at my outfit. I wore my one and only black pencil skirt; the one Sadie made me buy because she said I looked like a sexy librarian. Librarian, yes. Sexy, no. I paired it with a pale blue button-up blouse and my simple black pumps with the kitten heel. Looking toward my doorway, I see the jacket that matches the skirt hanging on a hook near the door. Slipping it on, I sigh in relief that I actually wore dressy business attire today. I'll look professional for this important meeting.

Before I take the elevator up two floors to the administration offices and conference room 3, I stop in the restroom to double-check my appearance. I wash my hands and run damp fingers through my stick-straight hair and push my bangs away from my eyes. Fortunately, I had the good sense to pull it back into a tight bun at the nape of my neck today. Some tidying up is all it needs. My make-up, what there is of it, is neutral and professional. I look down, once again, at my skirt, blouse, and black jacket and smile. Wow, this is my lucky day. I look *good*. It's like I had a feeling something big was happening today. I button the single button on the front of my jacket and give it tug, straightening it. "Deep breath, Agatha. You've got this."

As confidently as I can, I pull open the bathroom door and squeak in alarm as I run smack-dab into my co-working and office-bestie, Camille. "Oh, shoot, Cam. I'm sorry."

Laughing it off, Camille pats my shoulder. "No, it was my fault. I was reading a text instead of watching where I was going." Stepping around me she adds, "Want to do lunch today? I'm dying for a wrap from McGregor's."

"Sure. Well, maybe." I reach out and give her upper arm a squeeze. "I've got a meeting." I pause for dramatic effect. "Upstairs," I say excitedly.

"Oh, my God. Is it your promotion?" Camille says, hopping up and down.

"I think so. Finally," I roll my eyes but smile wide.

"You deserve it, honey. You work *so* hard."

"So do you." But the thing is, Camille hasn't been here as long as I have. She's not a CPA either. Someday I could see her moving up, just not yet.

"Nah, you deserve it." She moves further into the bathroom.

"Good luck. Be sure to stop in my cube when you get back. I want to hear *everything*."

Since our cubicles are next to each other, that's not a problem. "Okay. Talk to you soon."

"Good luck," she sing-songs just as the bathroom door shuts.

I walk to the elevator and press the UP button. Tugging my jacket once again, I repeat my mantra, "This is it, Agatha. Your life is about to change."

∼

Two Weeks Later

"Wake up, Agatha."

I hear a muffled voice that I just can't place.

"Aggie. Come on. Up and at 'em."

Atom? That's a funny word to use. I feel myself being gently jostled around.

"For fuck's sake, girl. Wake up!"

Wow, that one was loud and right next to my ear. I slowly open one eye to see two faces mere inches from mine.

"Wake the fuck up, woman." It's Keely. My baby sister has quite a mouth on her, that's for sure. "Where is my sister who wakes up at six in the morning, even on weekends? Huh?"

"She left the building," I mumble into the pillow.

Violet, her twin, is looking at me with furrowed brows and concern in her eyes. I open the other eye and stare for just a few more seconds. I need to think. I haven't quite figured out why they're here. Closing my eyes slowly, I do my best to remember what day it is. Friday? Is it Friday?

I push myself up a few inches, and then flop back down. I hurt. *Is it possible to get a hangover from cookie dough?*

"No, it's not. But if the number of empty wine boxes strewn

about your house is any indication of your night, I'd say cookie dough is *not* the culprit."

Shit. I said that aloud?

"Aggie, get up, damn it. You stink. When was the last time you showered?" There's a pause. "Or, hell, did anything like clean, dust, do the dishes, or vacuum your house? This place looks like a tornado whipped through here."

Keely Palmer. The baby of the family. She's the smallest and the loudest. The most outspoken of the bunch for sure. She doesn't mince words. Pushing myself up into a seated position, I look at my sisters again. "What time is it?"

"Jesus," mutters Keely. "It's after 3. In case your brain turned to mush in the last two weeks, which I suspect it has, that means it's the afternoon."

"Aggs?" Violet asks tentatively.

God. All I want to do is go back to sleep, but I can't. Sighing, I respond, "What, Vi?"

"You need to get up. Take a shower. Everyone will be here in an hour."

I sit up straight, "Everyone? Will be *here*?"

"Welcome to your very own intervention, big sis. Dad, Sadie, Lainie, and Keeton are all on their way, so you'd best jump up."

Shit. "B-but..."

"We let you wallow in self-pity for as long as we could, Agatha. Now crawl out of that disgusting bed and get in the shower. Vi and I will start cleaning up."

"Fine," I grumble. As I slide off the edge of the bed, I wince. Everything really does hurt. Yeah, maybe a shower is a good idea. You know, work out the kinks.

"Jesus." I turn to see Keely stripping the sheets off my bed. "What happened to the sister who changed her sheets twice a week, every Wednesday and Sunday, like an anal-retentive clock?"

I release a loud snort. She's funny. "She died," I mumble as I lumber to the bathroom and push open the door. As I enter, I glimpse the mess and wince again. "What the hell happened in here?" Clothes are strewn all over the floor and on top of the counter. To my right, an empty pizza box lays half on its side next to the bathtub. I spy a lone slice of pizza, mostly petrified, in the box. I stare at it for a second, trying to remember how it got there and how I missed that last slice. Squeezing my eyes shut, it comes to me. I ate pizza in the bathtub one night. The thing is, I'm not sure which night.

Stripping out of my shorts and tee, I reach in to turn the water on in my shower. Testing the temperature with my fingers, I adjust it before stepping in. As I do, I moan. *It feels so good.* How long's it been? Why does it seem like it was a year ago that I was canned from my job when it was only, what, two weeks ago? The truth is I haven't been completely sequestered. There was that time I got drunk with my sisters at Murphy's. Oh! What about the night I got drunk and met Lainie's new boyfriend, Keeton, at Keely and Lainie's place? See? I've been out. I stand under the warm spray for a good long while. It must have been too long because I'm startled to death when a surly Keely yanks back the shower curtain.

Holding a towel, she's tapping her foot on the ground like an angry headmistress. "Really?"

"What?" Seriously. What?

"You've been standing in there for like thirty minutes. That means you've got about thirty left to get this house in order before the rest of your family gets here. You do know what Lainie's going to do if she sees your place like this?"

Lainie is the eldest sister. She took on the role of mother when our own beloved mom died when I was eight. She was ten, too young to be a mommy. Her metamorphosis to mom happened gradually. "Yeah, okay. Let me get dressed and I'll be out." Keely's right, though. If Lainie sees my place like this and me looking like, well, like I'm depressed, she'll *literally* move in with me until I'm back to my happy-go-lucky self. No thanks. I've lived alone for most of my adult life. I like it. Don't get me wrong; I adore my sister, more than anything, but I love her more from across town. Distance and fondness and all that crap.

After quickly dressing in leggings and an Arizona State t-shirt, I run a brush over my teeth and another one through my hair. Searching my bathroom drawers, I spot a hair tie amongst some of my make-up. Pulling my hair up into a high ponytail, I stop and stare into the mirror. I look like shit. I'm pale, which makes the dark circles under my eyes more prominent. My eyes are puffy too; they look like I've gone ten rounds with Conor McGregor. No, not really, but you can tell I've been crying off and on for the last couple of weeks. I brush my bangs down in the hopes they'll hide half my face. I then contemplate whether I should dab on some make-up when Keely screams from the living room, "If you're not out here in ten seconds, I'm going to toss all one million of these pizza boxes out into your yard."

One million? She loves to exaggerate. I march out to the main room and spot Violet first. She's got a broom in her hand, sweeping my kitchen. I should be doing that. Movement to my right draws my attention back to Keely. She's standing near the front door with a stack of cardboard boxes. Pizza boxes. There are so many, I can't see her face at all. I quickly count them. *One, two, three, four, five, six, seven, eight.* "That's not a million."

"You've got one in your bathroom and two more in your bedroom. I'd say you're getting closer to the million-pizza mark."

"On a happy note, you've got enough coupons from the pizza boxes to get one free," says a cheery Violet.

Oh, sweet Violet.

But, truth? I may never be able to eat pizza again. Or drink Franzia Sunset Blush boxed wine ever, *ever* again. Peering around the room, I count three of those boxes in various places. "I'll get the wine boxes."

We spend the next thirty minutes frantically working to clean up my house, enough time to hide the evidence of my two-week wallowing bender. My dirty clothes are hidden in my closet. The pizza and wine boxes, numerous newspapers and magazines, and the equivalent of five boxes of Kleenex have all been tossed into the trash at the side of my house. I've lit one of my favorite candles and made us a pot of coffee. Just as I flop down on the sofa, a knock sounds on the door. "I'll get it," says Violet as she walks by.

When it opens, my dad steps in first. "Hey girls."

"Hi, Daddy." I say along with my two sisters. I stand up from the couch to meet him halfway. Kissing him on his cheek, I ask him if he wants a drink.

"Got any wine?" he asks.

"I, uh, I think I'm all out."

"No, you've got a box of something in your fridge," says Keely from the kitchen. "You want a glass too, Aggie?"

"N-no, thank you." I swallow hard. Just the thought of alcohol makes me feel queasy.

"How 'bout some cookie dough?" asks the smart ass.

"No, thanks."

Just then, my front door opens. I watch as Sadie, Lainie, and Keeton, Lainie's new boyfriend, step inside. I swallow hard when I see Keeton holding several boxes. Of pizza. The sight gives me a shiver.

"Ooh, pizza!" yells Keely, "Aggie's favorite."

Sister or not, just as soon as we're alone, I'm going to wring her scrawny neck.

My family is spread out all over my kitchen slash dining slash living room since no one room is large enough to contain all of us. Especially with our new addition, Keeton. The guy is mammoth. He's standing up next to my kitchen island, looking mighty uncomfortable. My house is small. Tiny, really. It's a two-bedroom bungalow but the second bedroom is so small, I'd categorize it as more of a closet or, on a good day, an office. I've got a small desk and chair in there along with an armoire for extra storage. That's about all that'll fit, to be honest. No worries; there's only me here, so it's the perfect size.

"So, Agatha," says my sister Lainie.

Here we go.

"Yes," I turn to face her. She's sitting in one of my two dining room chairs.

"How've you been?"

"Good."

"Have you sent out any resumes or found any jobs that sound promising?"

Wow, she cuts right to the chase. "Not yet." Pretending to be busy grabbing a slice of pizza, I bite into the ooey-gooey cheese and moan. Damn, I still love pizza.

"Have you checked out job listings?" asks Sadie.

"Not yet."

"Honey," says my dad, concern in his voice. "Will you please tell me what happened at H&S?"

Why hadn't my sisters told him? They blab everything to each other. *Everything.* I hate that about them, but the one time I need for them to blab to my dad, they don't. Traitors.

"I got fired."

"I know that, Agatha." Dad steps closer so he can sit beside me on the small sofa. Softly, he asks again. "Tell me what happened, honey."

Setting my slice down, I lean back on the sofa and look into my father's sweet eyes. I hate telling him. He doesn't deserve this. He's done his worrying. He's supposed to be enjoying life, not fretting about me, but I'm going to have to tell him.

"It'll feel good to talk it out." My dad is so wise.

"I got called into a meeting by Miriam, the human resources director. I thought I was finally getting promoted." I scoff. I'm becoming very jaded in my forced retirement.

"When I walked into the room, I realized Miriam wasn't alone. Drake Garlock, the CFO, and Trent Archer, the assistant Human Resources director, were at the table. My department head Kim Reynolds and Drake's administrative assistant, Monica, were also there."

I was surprised to see Drake in the room. The man dislikes me, but I don't know why. He had his trademark scowl on his face. I looked to Trent for some sort of reassurance but got none. In fact, he looked really nervous. He seemed to be more interested in the button on his jacket than on my promotion. When I looked at Miriam, she had no expression on her face whatsoever. I've always gotten along with Miriam. No, we didn't socialize or anything, but whenever I had a performance review, she was always pleasant. Even the times she had to tell me I was passed up for a promotion, she was nice. So, there I stood, waiting.

I looked at Dad. "Miriam asked me to sit down. So, I did." I lean forward on the sofa. "When I looked up, they all had angry expressions on their faces. Really angry. Especially Drake. He spoke first saying, 'Tell us why you did it.' I looked back at Drake, then at the others. I had no idea what he was talking about."

"Did you ask him what he meant?" asks Dad, moving to the edge of his seat, literally.

"I did, but he just laughed, or scoffed, I guess, is a better word. Miriam spoke next. She said, 'We know you took the money.' I must have looked horrified or something because Miriam sat back suddenly. 'What money?' I asked. Then Trent piped up, 'You know what money.' I turned to him next and said, 'No, Trent, I don't.'"

I feel a tear slide down my cheek and quickly wipe it away. I don't like thinking about this and especially about Trent and the look of disgust on his face. I thought Trent and I... well, I thought he and I were going to be something. But not anymore.

"Keep going, Aggie. We didn't get to hear any of this either. You only told us the abridged version at Murphy's," says Lainie.

I'd met my sisters at Murphy's the day I was fired and told them some of this, but not all of it. I couldn't do it then. Hell, it's hard now—two weeks later.

"Well, there were some other things said. I'm not sure I remember the words exactly but, essentially, they said I'd embezzled over one hundred thousand dollars over a four-year period."

"A hundred thousand dollars?" chokes my father.

"Yeah. That's what they claimed."

"Did they tell you how you did it?" Keeton has moved closer to the conversation. I'm sure he knew the basic story from Lainie.

"No. They just said that I took the money, that they knew I took the money, and that they wanted me to sign a non-disclosure agreement and leave the premises immediately. If I did, they wouldn't press charges."

"Now, that's the part that gets me," says Sadie. "That's a shit-ton of money. Why wouldn't they have you arrested?"

"Gee, thanks, Sadie," I reply glumly.

"No, I just mean..."

"If it's a publicly-traded company, they'd want to keep it on the down-low," replies Keeton. "Stocks would be impacted at that news."

"It is public. The other reason would be to keep it out of the press," says Violet. "Bad for business."

"Did you try to defend yourself?" asks Keely. "Did you fight?"

"I told them I was innocent."

"What happened then?" Sadie asks, sitting on the back of my sofa. My entire family is all around me now.

I blush, thinking about what happened next. "I, uh, signed the NDA and I stood to leave..."

They all stare at me. The room is silent for a beat when Violet speaks. "Keep going, Aggs. Tell us the rest."

It just hit me, I'm not even supposed to talk about it with my family thanks to the NDA. "You guys can't tell anyone any of this."

"Honey, of course we won't," says my dad as he pats my knee. "Keep going."

"Okay. Well, Drake told the security guys to escort me to my desk, and to make sure I only took my personal belongings, and to show me the door."

And they did that. I felt like I was a dead man walking through the office. Everyone stared at the three of us. I'm sure no one knew what was happening but by the tears running down my cheeks, they had to know something was amiss.

"Security guys? What security guys?" Lainie asks, surprised.

"Oh, there were two security guys there. I hadn't noticed them when I walked in and I'd never seen them before."

"Security or *cops*?" snaps Keely. She's got a thing about cops. The thing? She doesn't like them.

"Security? I think. I'm not sure."

"Keep going, honey. You're almost done," Dad says squeezing my hand, "It's good for you to let this all out."

"They walked me to my desk. One of the guys was kind of gruff so the other one sent him off to do something else saying, 'I got this.' The older one helped me pack up a box with my things and then he walked me to the elevator and down to the ground floor and out to the street. That was it."

I can't tell my family that I sobbed the entire eleven floors down. It's embarrassing. In my defense, I did it quietly. The security guy was nice enough to carry my box for me until we got outside. He set it down on the sidewalk in front of me. Just as I was about to leave, I looked at him, for the first time, really. He was handsome, ruggedly handsome, but those thoughts were for another time, another place. Anyway, I looked into his clear, blue eyes and said with a shaky voice, "I—" I paused, trying to put the words together. "I did *not* take that money."

Without a word from him, I picked up my box, turned, and walked down the street. Away from a career I loved, well liked a lot. I guess I should have been happy. I had my freedom.

www.ingramcontent.com/pod-product-compliance
Lightning Source LLC
Chambersburg PA
CBHW020408080526
44584CB00014B/1223